ALASKA

travel guide

ALASKA
Travel Guide

2025

Essential tips for exploring the last frontier with ease

TONY MARK

COPYRIGHT

Table of contents

Anchorage

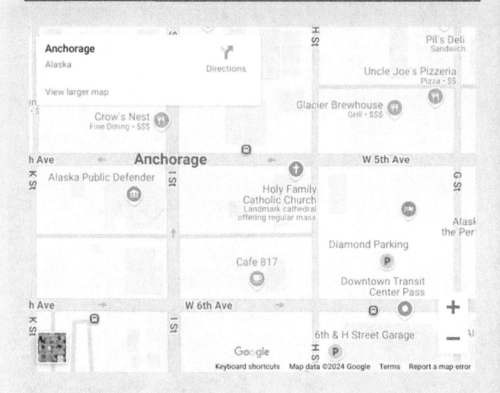

SCAN THE QR CODE

- Open your device's camera app
- Point the camera at the QR code
- Ensure the QR code is within the frame and well-lit
- Wait for your device to recognize the QR code
- Once recognized, tap on the map and input for current location for direction and distance to the destination

There's an entire section filled with interactive maps

Fairbanks

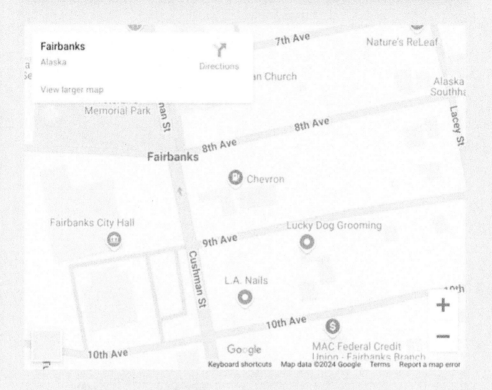

SCAN THE QR CODE

- Open your device's camera app
- Point the camera at the QR code
- Ensure the QR code is within the frame and well-lit
- Wait for your device to recognize the QR code
- Once recognized, tap on the map and input for current location for direction and distance to the destination

There's an entire section filled with interactive maps

Juneau

SCAN THE QR CODE

- Open your device's camera app
- Point the camera at the QR code
- Ensure the QR code is within the frame and well-lit
- Wait for your device to recognize the QR code
- Once recognized, tap on the map and input for current location for direction and distance to the destination

There's an entire section filled with interactive maps

INTRODUCTION

So, you're thinking about Alaska, huh? Good choice. It's wild, it's beautiful, and it's totally unlike anywhere else. Let's get this adventure started.

Welcome to the Last Frontier

Imagine a place where glaciers calve into the sea with a thunderous roar, where grizzlies fish for salmon in crystal-clear streams, and where the Northern Lights paint the sky with an ethereal dance of color. Welcome to Alaska, a land of untamed wilderness, breathtaking beauty, and endless adventure.

Here, the rhythm of life is dictated by the seasons, the tides, and the migration of wildlife. It's a place where you can feel truly connected to nature, where the vastness of the landscape humbles you, and where the silence is broken only by the call of a loon or the crackle of a campfire.

Alaska is not just another destination; it's an experience that will awaken your senses, challenge your limits, and leave an indelible mark on your soul. It's a place where you can escape the hustle and bustle of everyday life and discover a world that is both ancient and awe-inspiring.

What sets Alaska apart?

- **Untouched wilderness:** Alaska boasts vast expanses of pristine wilderness, from towering mountains and glaciers to sprawling tundra and dense forests. It's a haven for wildlife and a playground for outdoor enthusiasts.
- **Epic landscapes**: Prepare to be awestruck by Alaska's dramatic scenery, from the majestic peaks of Denali National Park to the breathtaking fjords of Kenai Fjords National Park. Every turn reveals a new vista that will leave you speechless.
- **Abundant wildlife:** Alaska is teeming with wildlife, from brown bears and moose to humpback whales and bald eagles. You'll have the chance to witness these magnificent creatures in their natural habitat, creating unforgettable memories.
- **Rich cultural heritage:** Alaska is home to diverse indigenous cultures, each with its own unique traditions and art forms. Immerse yourself in their fascinating history and experience the warmth of their hospitality

- **Adventure at every turn:** Whether you're hiking through glaciers, kayaking among icebergs, or dog sledding across snowy landscapes, Alaska offers endless opportunities for adventure and exploration.
- **The Northern Lights:** Witness the mesmerizing dance of the aurora borealis, a natural phenomenon that illuminates the night sky with vibrant colors. It's a spectacle that will leave you in awe of nature's power and beauty.

Alaska is not just a destination; it's a journey of self-discovery. It's a place where you can reconnect with nature, challenge yourself, and create memories that will last a lifetime. So pack your bags, leave your worries behind, and prepare to embark on the adventure of a lifetime in the Last Frontier.

Why Alaska Should Be Your Next Destination

Witness Nature's Masterpieces: Alaska is a canvas painted with breathtaking landscapes that defy imagination. Towering glaciers, pristine fjords, snow-capped peaks, and endless stretches of wilderness create a visual symphony that will leave you breathless.

- **Encounter the Wild:** Experience the thrill of observing Alaska's iconic wildlife in their natural habitat. Watch brown bears fish for salmon, witness humpback whales breach in icy waters, and listen to the haunting call of wolves echoing through the valleys. Alaska is a wildlife lover's paradise.

- **Embrace the Spirit of Adventure**: Alaska is a playground for outdoor enthusiasts. Hike through breathtaking trails, kayak among icebergs, embark on a scenic train journey, or witness the mesmerizing dance of the Northern Lights. The possibilities for adventure are limitless.

- **Immerse Yourself in Rich Culture**: Discover the vibrant traditions and art forms of Alaska's indigenous peoples. Visit cultural centers, witness traditional dances, and learn about their deep connection to the land. Alaska offers a unique opportunity to experience living cultures that have thrived for centuries.

- **Escape the Ordinary:** Leave the crowds and concrete jungles behind. Alaska offers a true escape, a chance to disconnect from the everyday and reconnect with nature's grandeur. Breathe in the fresh air, feel the silence of the wilderness, and experience a sense of peace that is hard to find elsewhere.

- **Create Memories that Last a Lifetime:** Alaska is a destination that will leave an indelible mark on your heart. The experiences you have, the people you meet, and the natural wonders you witness will stay with you long after you leave. Alaska is a journey that transforms, inspires, and awakens the spirit of adventure within.

Whether you seek tranquility, adventure, or a deeper connection with nature, Alaska promises an unforgettable experience that will leave you longing to return.

How to Use This Guide

This guide is designed to be your trusted companion as you plan and embark on your Alaskan adventure. We've crafted it with your needs in mind, ensuring it's both informative and easy to use. Here's how to make the most of this guide:

Structure & Organization:
- **Chapter-by-Chapter Breakdown**: We've divided the guide into logical chapters, each focusing on a key aspect of your trip. From planning and logistics to exploring specific regions and engaging in various activities, you'll find all the information you need in a clear and organized manner.
- **Table of Contents & Index**: Use the detailed Table of Contents at the beginning and the comprehensive Index at the end to quickly locate specific topics or areas of interest.
- **Visual Cues:** Throughout the guide, we've incorporated maps, photos, and other visual aids to enhance your understanding and inspire your wanderlust.

Catering to Diverse Travel Styles:
- **Itineraries for Every Interest**: Whether you're an intrepid adventurer, a culture enthusiast, a family with kids, or a budget-conscious traveler, we've included sample itineraries tailored to your preferences.

These itineraries provide a starting point for planning your trip, and you can customize them to fit your specific interests and time constraints.

- **Activity Recommendations**: We've included a wide range of activities and experiences, from hiking and wildlife viewing to cultural immersion and scenic train journeys. You'll find options suitable for all ages, fitness levels, and interests.
- **Practical Tips:** We've sprinkled practical tips and insider advice throughout the guide, ensuring you're well-prepared for your Alaskan adventure. From packing lists and safety tips to budgeting advice and cultural etiquette, we've got you covered.

User-Friendly Features:
- **Clear & Concise Language:** We've avoided jargon and technical terms, ensuring the information is accessible and easy to understand.
- **Insider Tips:** We've included insider tips and local recommendations to help you discover hidden gems and experience Alaska like a true insider.
- **Inspiring Stories:** We've woven in personal anecdotes and stories from fellow travelers to bring Alaska to life and ignite your imagination.

Whether you're a seasoned traveler or embarking on your first Alaskan adventure, this guide is your key to unlocking the wonders of the Last Frontier. Let it be your inspiration, your source of knowledge, and your trusted companion as you create memories that will last a lifetime.

CHAPTER 1

Planning Your Alaskan Adventure

O Okay, dreamer, time to turn those Alaska daydreams into a real plan. Deep breath, let's tackle the logistics first....

When to Visit: A Season-by-Season Breakdown

Alaska's dramatic seasons offer unique experiences throughout the year. Here's a detailed breakdown of each season to help you decide the perfect time for your dream Alaskan adventure:

Summer (June - August)
- **Weather:** Long, sunny days with mild temperatures, averaging between 50°F to 70°F (10°C to 21°C). Southeast Alaska experiences more rainfall, while Southcentral and Interior regions are drier.
- **Daylight:** The "Land of the Midnight Sun" lives up to its name, with some areas experiencing nearly 24 hours of daylight, providing ample time for exploration and outdoor activities.
- **Wildlife:** This is peak season for wildlife viewing. Expect to witness bears feasting on salmon, whales breaching in coastal waters, moose grazing in meadows, and eagles soaring overhead.

- **Popular Events:** Summer solstice celebrations, fishing derbies, music festivals, and outdoor concerts fill the calendar, adding a festive touch to your trip.
- **Considerations:** Peak season also brings higher prices and larger crowds. Book accommodations and tours well in advance, especially for popular destinations like Denali National Park.

Shoulder Seasons (May & September)
- **Weather:** Transition months offer milder temperatures than summer, ranging from 40°F to 60°F (4°C to 15°C). May can still have lingering snow, while September brings crisp air and the start of the stunning fall foliage.
- **Daylight:** Daylight hours decrease gradually, offering a balance between outdoor activities and opportunities for Northern Lights viewing, especially in September.
- **Wildlife**: Wildlife is still active, though some species may begin their migration or hibernation preparations. It's a great time for birdwatching as migratory birds pass through.
- **Popular Events:** Enjoy fall foliage festivals, witness the awe-inspiring bird migration, and participate in early-season winter activities like dog sledding.
- **Considerations:** Some businesses and tours may operate on reduced schedules or be closed during shoulder seasons. Check availability in advance, particularly in remote areas.

Winter (October - April)
- **Weather:** Cold and snowy, with temperatures ranging from -20°F to 30°F (-29°C to -1°C). Interior regions are significantly colder and experience shorter days than coastal areas.
- **Daylight**: Daylight is limited, with some areas experiencing only a few hours of sunlight per day. However, the long nights create ideal conditions for witnessing the mesmerizing Aurora Borealis.
- **Wildlife:** Some animals migrate or hibernate, but you can still spot hardy creatures like moose, caribou, and wolves. Winter is also prime time for dog sledding, snowmobiling, and ice fishing.

- **Popular Events:** Experience the excitement of the Iditarod Trail Sled Dog Race, celebrate the Fur Rendezvous Festival, and witness the artistry of the World Ice Art Championships.
- **Considerations**: Pack for cold weather with warm layers, waterproof boots, and gloves. Some roads and attractions may be closed or have limited access during winter.

Best Time to Visit Based on Your Interests:
- **Wildlife Viewing:** Summer is ideal, but shoulder seasons (especially September) offer fantastic opportunities with fewer crowds.
- **Northern Lights:** Winter and shoulder seasons (particularly September and March) provide the best chances to witness the Aurora Borealis.
- **Hiking and Backpacking:** Summer and early fall offer the most accessible trails and pleasant temperatures.
- **Winter Activities:** Embrace the snow and cold during winter for skiing, snowboarding, dog sledding, snowmobiling, and ice fishing.
- **Photography:** Summer provides long daylight hours and vibrant landscapes, while winter captures the magic of snow-covered scenery and the Northern Lights.

- **Budget Travel:** Shoulder seasons generally have lower prices and fewer crowds than the peak summer months.

No matter when you choose to visit, Alaska promises an unforgettable journey. By aligning your trip with your interests and desired experiences, you'll create memories that last a lifetime in this awe-inspiring land.

Getting There: Air, Sea, or Road?

Embarking on your Alaskan adventure begins with choosing the best way to reach this remote and captivating destination. Here's a breakdown of the primary transportation options, along with tips for finding the best deals and planning your journey:

By Air
Pros:
- Fastest option, especially for long-distance travelers.
- Major airports in Anchorage, Fairbanks, and Juneau offer connections to various cities within Alaska and the Lower 48.
- Convenient for reaching remote areas and national parks via smaller connecting flights.

Cons:
- Can be expensive, especially during peak season.
- Limits opportunities for scenic views during the journey itself.

Tips for Finding Deals:
- **Book in advance:** Airfare tends to increase closer to the travel date, so book early, especially for summer travel.
- **Be flexible with dates:** Consider traveling during shoulder seasons (May or September) or weekdays for potential savings.
- **Use flight comparison websites:** Compare fares across multiple airlines using websites like Kayak, Skyscanner, or Google Flights.
- **Sign up for airline newsletters and fare alerts:** Stay informed about special offers and promotions.
- **Consider flying into smaller airports:** Sometimes, flying into a smaller airport near your destination can be cheaper, even with the added cost of ground transportation.

By Cruise Ship
Pros:
- A relaxing and scenic way to experience Alaska's coastline, glaciers, and wildlife.
- Offers a variety of onboard activities and amenities.
- Convenient for visiting multiple destinations without the hassle of packing and unpacking.

Cons:
- Can be more expensive than other options, especially for luxury cruises.
- Limited time in each port of call.
- May not provide access to Alaska's interior and remote areas.

Tips for Finding Deals:
- **Book early or last-minute:** Cruise lines often offer discounts for early bookings or last-minute deals to fill unsold cabins.
- **Consider shoulder seasons:** Cruises during May or September can be less crowded and more affordable.

- **Look for repositioning cruises:** These cruises occur when ships are moving between their summer and winter homeports, often offering lower fares.
- **Compare cruise lines and itineraries:** Research different cruise lines and their itineraries to find the best fit for your interests and budget.
- **Utilize a travel agent**: A travel agent specializing in cruises can help you find the best deals and provide valuable insights.

By Road (Alaska Highway)
Pros:
- A scenic and adventurous road trip through Canada and Alaska.
- Offers flexibility and the freedom to explore at your own pace.
- Potentially more affordable than flying or cruising, especially for groups or families.

Cons:
- Requires a significant time commitment, with the drive from the Lower 48 taking several days.
- Can be challenging, especially during winter months, with potential for road closures and wildlife encounters.
- Limited access to some remote areas and islands.

Tips for Planning a Road Trip:
- **Plan your route carefully:** Research road conditions, distances, and attractions along the way.
- **Allow ample time:** Don't rush the journey. Factor in time for scenic stops, wildlife viewing, and unexpected delays.
- **Book accommodations in advance:** Especially during peak season, campgrounds and hotels can fill up quickly.
- **Prepare your vehicle:** Ensure your vehicle is in good condition and equipped for long distances and potentially challenging road conditions.
- **Be aware of wildlife:** Drive cautiously and be prepared for encounters with moose, bears, and other animals.

Choosing Your Alaskan Base: Anchorage, Fairbanks, or Juneau?

Selecting the right base for your Alaskan adventure can significantly impact your overall experience. Each of Alaska's major cities offers unique attractions, accessibility to different regions, and distinct vibes. Let's explore their characteristics to help you decide which city best aligns with your interests and travel style:

Anchorage: The Urban Hub

- **Accessibility:** As Alaska's largest city, Anchorage boasts an international airport with numerous flight connections. It's also the starting point for the scenic Alaska Railroad and a major hub for car rentals.
- **Attractions:** Discover a blend of urban amenities and natural beauty. Explore the Alaska Wildlife Conservation Center, hike in Chugach State Park, or immerse yourself in the rich culture at the Alaska Native Heritage Center.

- **Surrounding Areas**: Gateway to Kenai Peninsula, home to Kenai Fjords National Park, abundant wildlife, and opportunities for fishing, kayaking, and glacier trekking.

Best For:
- First-time visitors seeking a mix of urban comforts and outdoor adventures.
- Travelers with limited time who want to experience a variety of attractions within a reasonable distance.
- Families looking for a balance of kid-friendly activities and natural exploration.

Fairbanks: The Golden Heart City
- **Accessibility:** Fairbanks International Airport offers convenient access, and the Alaska Highway provides a scenic road trip option. It's also the terminus of the Alaska Railroad.
- **Attractions:** Immerse yourself in the gold rush history at Pioneer Park, witness the Northern Lights at the University of Alaska Museum of the North, or experience the natural hot springs at Chena Hot Springs Resort.
- **Surrounding Areas:** Explore the vast Interior region, including Denali National Park, the Arctic Circle, and charming towns like Talkeetna.

Best For:
- Adventurous travelers seeking a more remote and authentic Alaskan experience.
- Northern Lights enthusiasts, as Fairbanks offers prime viewing opportunities due to its location.
- Those interested in gold rush history and Alaska's unique interior landscapes.

Juneau: The Capital City Surrounded by Wilderness
- **Accessibility:** Accessible primarily by air or sea, with regular flights and cruise ship arrivals. The Alaska Marine Highway ferry system connects Juneau to other coastal communities.

- **Attractions:** Visit the majestic Mendenhall Glacier, explore the historic downtown area, or take a whale-watching tour in the scenic waters of the Inside Passage.
- **Surrounding Areas**: Discover the breathtaking beauty of Glacier Bay National Park, accessible by boat or small plane from Juneau. Explore nearby islands and coastal communities for a taste of Alaskan island life.

Best For:
- Nature lovers seeking close encounters with glaciers, whales, and other marine life.
- Those interested in experiencing Alaska's coastal beauty and island culture.
- Travelers who enjoy a mix of outdoor adventure and city exploration.

Ultimately, the best base for your Alaskan adventure depends on your individual preferences, interests, and travel style. Consider the following factors when making your decision:

- Priorities: What are your must-see attractions and experiences?
- Accessibility: How do you plan to travel within Alaska?
- Time: How much time do you have for your trip?
- Budget: What is your travel budget?
- Travel Style: Do you prefer a more urban or remote experience?

By carefully considering these factors and exploring the unique characteristics of each city, you'll be well on your way to choosing the perfect Alaskan base for an unforgettable journey.

Accommodation Options: From Rustic Cabins to Luxury Lodges

Alaska offers a wide range of accommodation options to suit every budget and travel style, from cozy cabins nestled in the wilderness to luxurious lodges with breathtaking views. Here's a glimpse into the diverse lodging landscape of the Last Frontier:

Budget-Friendly Havens:

- **Hostels:** A great choice for solo travelers and backpackers seeking affordable accommodation and social interaction. Hostels are typically located in major cities and offer shared dorms and communal spaces.
- **Campgrounds:** Experience Alaska's natural beauty firsthand by pitching a tent or parking your RV in one of the many campgrounds scattered across the state. Remember to follow bear safety guidelines and be prepared for potential wildlife encounters.
- **Budget Hotels and Motels:** Find comfortable and affordable rooms in towns and cities throughout Alaska. These options provide basic amenities and a convenient base for exploring the surrounding areas.

Mid-Range Retreats:

- **Cabins and Vacation Rentals:** Enjoy a more secluded and personalized experience by renting a cabin or vacation home. These options offer a home-away-from-home feeling, often with fully equipped kitchens and scenic views.
- **Historic Hotels and Lodges:** Step back in time and experience the charm of Alaska's past by staying in a historic hotel or lodge. Many of these properties boast unique architecture, antique furnishings, and a sense of old-world elegance.

- **Wilderness Lodges:** Immerse yourself in the wilderness by staying in a lodge nestled amidst breathtaking scenery. These lodges offer comfortable accommodations, delicious meals, and guided activities, allowing you to experience Alaska's natural wonders firsthand.

Luxury Escapes:
- **Luxury Lodges and Resorts:** Indulge in the ultimate Alaskan experience by staying in a luxurious lodge or resort. These properties offer top-notch amenities, personalized service, gourmet dining, and stunning views.
- **Cruise Ship Accommodations:** Combine transportation and accommodation by choosing a cruise ship for your Alaskan adventure. Cruise ships offer a variety of cabin options, from cozy interior rooms to spacious suites with private balconies.
- **Fly-In Lodges:** Access remote and exclusive wilderness areas by staying in a fly-in lodge. These lodges offer unparalleled access to fishing, hiking, wildlife viewing, and other outdoor activities in pristine settings.

Booking Accommodations:
- **Peak Season (June-August):** Book well in advance, especially for popular destinations and lodges. Consider alternative dates or shoulder seasons for more availability and potentially lower prices.
- **Remote Areas:** Lodges and accommodations in remote areas often have limited capacity and may require advanced booking or special transportation arrangements.
- **Online Booking Platforms:** Utilize online travel agencies and booking platforms to compare prices, read reviews, and find the best deals.
- **Direct Bookings:** Contact lodges and hotels directly to inquire about availability and special offers, especially for smaller, independent properties.

Popular Hotels in Alaska:
- **Alyeska Resort:** A luxurious ski resort in Girdwood with stunning mountain views, an aerial tram, and a variety of dining options.

The Lakefront Anchorage: A modern hotel in downtown Anchorage with spacious rooms, scenic views, and easy access to attractions.

Pike's Waterfront Lodge: A charming lodge in Fairbanks overlooking the Chena River, offering comfortable rooms, a popular restaurant, and convenient access to outdoor activities.

Harbor 360 Hotel: A waterfront hotel in Seward with breathtaking views of Resurrection Bay and the surrounding mountains.

Land's End Resort: A relaxed resort in Homer with cozy rooms and lodges, an indoor pool, and stunning views of Kachemak Bay.

Chena Hot Springs Resort: A unique resort near Fairbanks featuring natural hot springs, an ice museum, and opportunities for Northern Lights viewing.

Denali Park Hotel: A comfortable hotel near Denali National Park, offering convenient access to park activities and breathtaking views.

Westmark Fairbanks Hotel and Conference Center: A centrally located hotel in Fairbanks with modern amenities and easy access to downtown attractions.

Mt. McKinley Princess Wilderness Lodge: A rustic lodge near Denali National Park, offering a true Alaskan wilderness experience with comfortable accommodations and guided activities.

Grande Denali Lodge: A luxurious lodge with panoramic views of Denali National Park, offering upscale amenities, fine dining, and guided excursions.

No matter your budget or travel style, Alaska offers a range of accommodations to ensure a comfortable and memorable stay. With careful planning and research, you'll find the perfect place to rest your head and experience the magic of the Last Frontier.

Transportation Within Alaska: Navigating the Vast Landscape

Exploring Alaska's vast and diverse landscapes requires careful consideration of transportation options. Each method offers unique advantages and challenges, and the best choice for you will depend on your itinerary, budget, and desired experiences.

Here's a breakdown of the primary transportation methods within Alaska, along with tips for navigating its unique challenges:

Rental Cars:

Pros:

- Flexibility and freedom to explore at your own pace.
- Ideal for road trips and accessing remote areas with well-maintained roads.
- Convenient for carrying luggage and gear.

Cons:

- Can be expensive, especially during peak season.
- Limited to areas with road access, excluding many remote regions and islands.
- Requires careful driving due to wildlife, changing weather, and long distances between towns.

Tips for Navigating Alaska's Roads:

- Plan your routes carefully: Research road conditions, distances, and potential closures.
- Allow ample time: Distances can be deceiving, so factor in extra time for scenic stops and unexpected delays.
- Be prepared for wildlife: Drive cautiously and be aware of moose, bears, and other animals crossing the road.
- Check weather conditions: Be prepared for changing weather, especially in mountainous areas.
- Fuel up frequently: Gas stations can be sparse in remote areas, so fill up whenever possible.

The Alaska Railroad:

Pros:

- A scenic and relaxing way to travel between major cities and national parks.
- Offers comfortable seating, dining options, and stunning views.
- Convenient for accessing Denali National Park and other popular destinations along the rail line.

Cons:

- Limited routes and schedules compared to other transportation options.
- Can be more expensive than driving or taking the ferry.
- May not provide access to remote areas or off-the-beaten-path destinations.

Tips for Planning a Scenic Train Journey:

- **Book early:** Especially during peak season, popular routes and times can sell out quickly.
- **Consider a multi-day package:** Combine train travel with accommodations and activities for a seamless experience.
- **Choose the right class of service:** Options range from standard coach seats to luxurious GoldStar service with panoramic views and fine dining.
- **Pack snacks and drinks:** While food and beverages are available onboard, bringing your own can save money and offer more choices.
- **Take advantage of onboard activities:** Many trains offer ranger-led programs, live music, and other entertainment options.

Ferries (Alaska Marine Highway System):

Pros:

- A scenic and affordable way to explore Alaska's coastal communities and islands.
- Offers various vessel types, from smaller passenger ferries to larger car ferries.
- Provides opportunities for wildlife viewing and breathtaking scenery.

Cons:

- Can be time-consuming, with longer travel times than flying or driving.
- Schedules can be affected by weather conditions and seasonal changes.
- Limited access to interior regions and certain remote areas.

Tips for Ferry Travel:
- Check schedules and book in advance: Ferry schedules can change, so check the latest information and book your passage early, especially during peak season.
- Consider cabin accommodations: For longer journeys or overnight travel, consider booking a cabin for added comfort and privacy.
- Pack for all weather: Even in summer, temperatures can drop on the water, so bring layers and rain gear.
- Bring your own food and drinks: While food is available onboard, bringing your own can save money and offer more choices.
- Take advantage of onboard amenities: Many ferries offer observation decks, lounges, and even movie theaters.

Small Planes and Bush Flights:

Pros:
- Access remote areas and national parks not accessible by road or ferry.
- Offer stunning aerial views of Alaska's landscapes.
- Ideal for short trips, day excursions, and accessing fly-in lodges.

Cons:
- Can be expensive compared to other transportation options.
- Weather dependent, with potential for delays or cancellations.
- Limited luggage capacity on smaller planes.

Tips for Choosing a Bush Flight:
- **Research reputable operators**: Choose a company with a good safety record and experienced pilots.
- **Book in advance:** Especially during peak season, flights can fill up quickly.
- **Be flexible with your schedule:** Weather conditions can impact flight schedules, so be prepared for potential delays.
- **Pack light**: Luggage restrictions apply, so pack only essentials.
- **Enjoy the views:** Take advantage of the unique aerial perspective and capture stunning photos.

CHAPTER 2

Unveiling Alaska's Natural Wonders

G et ready to have your mind blown. Alaska's landscapes are the kind that make you feel tiny, but in the best possible way.

Denali National Park: Home to North America's Highest Peak

Encompassing over six million acres of pristine wilderness, Denali National Park is a testament to nature's grandeur.

Its landscapes range from the towering heights of Mount Denali (formerly Mount McKinley), North America's tallest peak, to the vast expanse of the tundra, teeming with wildlife. Prepare to be captivated by the park's diverse ecosystems and the abundant opportunities for adventure.

Diverse Landscapes:
- **The Alaska Range:** This majestic mountain range dominates the park's skyline, with Denali's snow-capped summit reaching an awe-inspiring 20,310 feet. The surrounding peaks create a dramatic backdrop for hiking, camping, and wildlife viewing.

- **Tundra:** Stretching across vast distances, the tundra is a seemingly endless carpet of low-lying vegetation, dotted with wildflowers in the summer months. It's a crucial habitat for caribou, Dall sheep, and other wildlife.
- **Boreal Forest:** Spruce, birch, and aspen trees blanket the lower elevations, providing shelter for moose, bears, and a variety of bird species. Explore the forest trails for a chance to encounter these creatures in their natural habitat.
- **Glaciers and Rivers:** Denali boasts numerous glaciers and braided rivers, carving their way through the landscape and creating stunning vistas. Witness the power of nature as glaciers calve into turquoise lakes or embark on a scenic rafting trip down a glacial river.

Exploring Denali:
- **Bus Tours:** The park's 92-mile Denali Park Road offers access to the heart of the wilderness. Hop on a narrated bus tour for a chance to see wildlife, learn about the park's history and ecosystems, and capture breathtaking photos. Various tour options cater to different interests and time constraints, from shorter Tundra Wilderness Tours to the full-day Kantishna Experience.
- **Hiking Trails**: Denali offers a vast network of trails, from easy walks to challenging backcountry treks. Popular options include the Savage River Loop Trail, the Horseshoe Lake Trail, and the Mount Healy Overlook Trail. Remember to be bear aware and follow park regulations when hiking in Denali.
- **Wildlife Viewing:** Denali is renowned for its abundant wildlife, including grizzly bears, moose, caribou, wolves, and Dall sheep. The best opportunities for viewing occur along the Denali Park Road, especially in the early morning or evening hours. Consider joining a guided wildlife tour for expert insights and increased chances of spotting elusive creatures.

Additional Activities:
- **Backpacking:** Experience the solitude and beauty of Denali's backcountry by embarking on a multi-day backpacking trip. Obtain necessary permits and be prepared for challenging terrain and unpredictable weather.

- **Camping:** Several campgrounds within the park offer a chance to sleep under the stars and immerse yourself in the wilderness. Reservations are highly recommended, especially during peak season.
- **Flightseeing:** Take to the skies for a breathtaking aerial perspective of Denali's majestic landscapes. Flightseeing tours offer a unique way to appreciate the park's vastness and witness its glaciers, mountains, and wildlife from above.

Tips for Visiting Denali:
- **Plan Ahead:** Denali is a popular destination, so book accommodations, bus tours, and other activities well in advance, especially during peak season (June-August).
- **Be Prepared for Weather:** Weather in Denali can change quickly, so pack layers and be prepared for rain, snow, or sunshine.
- **Respect Wildlife:** Maintain a safe distance from animals and follow park regulations to ensure both your safety and the well-being of the wildlife.
- **Embrace the Experience**: Denali offers a unique opportunity to connect with nature and witness its raw beauty. Take time to appreciate the silence, the vastness, and the incredible creatures that call this park home.

Kenai Fjords National Park: Where Glaciers Meet the Sea

Prepare to be mesmerized by the breathtaking beauty of Kenai Fjords National Park, a glacial wonderland where towering ice formations meet the rugged coastline, creating a dramatic and awe-inspiring landscape. This park is a haven for wildlife and a playground for outdoor enthusiasts, offering unforgettable experiences amidst some of Alaska's most stunning scenery.

Glaciers, Fjords, and Marine Life:

- **Harding Icefield:** The park's centerpiece is the Harding Icefield, a vast expanse of ice covering over 700 square miles. This massive icefield feeds numerous glaciers that flow down to the sea, carving deep fjords and creating dramatic waterfalls along the way.
- **Tidewater Glaciers:** Witness the power of nature as massive tidewater glaciers, like Aialik Glacier and Northwestern Glacier, calve into the ocean, creating thunderous booms and sending waves rippling through the water.
- **Fjords:** Explore the park's intricate network of fjords, deep U-shaped valleys carved by glaciers over thousands of years.

- **Marine Life:** Keep your eyes peeled for humpback whales, orcas, sea otters, puffins, and a variety of other marine mammals and seabirds that thrive in the nutrient-rich waters of Kenai Fjords.

Recommended Activities:
- **Boat Tours:** Embark on a boat tour to witness the park's highlights, including glaciers, fjords, and abundant wildlife. Several tour operators offer a variety of options, ranging from half-day cruises to multi-day excursions with overnight stays in remote lodges.
- **Kayaking:** Paddle through the calm waters of the fjords, getting up close and personal with glaciers and marine life. Guided kayaking tours cater to different skill levels and provide all necessary equipment and safety instructions.
- **Hiking:** Explore the park's trails, which range from easy walks to challenging climbs. The Harding Icefield Trail offers spectacular views of the icefield and surrounding mountains, while the Exit Glacier Trail leads to the edge of a retreating glacier.

Trails with Breathtaking Views:
- **Harding Icefield Trail:** This strenuous 8.2-mile (round trip) trail climbs steeply to the edge of the Harding Icefield, rewarding hikers with panoramic views of glaciers, mountains, and the vast expanse of ice.
- **Exit Glacier Trail:** This accessible 2-mile (round trip) trail winds through lush forest to the foot of Exit Glacier, showcasing the effects of climate change on this receding ice formation.
- **Resurrection Pass Trail:** This challenging 38-mile (one way) trail traverses the Kenai Mountains, offering stunning views of alpine lakes, waterfalls, and glaciers. Ideal for experienced backpackers seeking a multi-day adventure.

Tips for Visiting Kenai Fjords:
- **Book Tours in Advance:** Popular boat tours and kayaking excursions fill up quickly, especially during peak season. Reserve your spot early to avoid disappointment.

- **Dress in Layers:** Be prepared for changing weather conditions, especially on boat tours and hikes. Dress in layers and bring rain gear, even in summer.
- **Bring Binoculars and a Camera:** These essential tools will enhance your wildlife viewing and help you capture the park's stunning scenery.
- **Respect Wildlife:** Maintain a safe distance from animals and follow park regulations to ensure both your safety and the well-being of the wildlife.
- **Embrace the Experience:** Kenai Fjords National Park offers a unique opportunity to witness the raw power and beauty of nature. Take time to appreciate the silence, the vastness, and the intricate ecosystems that thrive in this remarkable landscape.

Whether you choose to explore by boat, kayak, or foot, Kenai Fjords National Park promises an unforgettable adventure that will leave you in awe of Alaska's natural wonders.

Glacier Bay National Park: Awe-Inspiring Tidewater Glaciers

Glacier Bay National Park is a living testament to the awe-inspiring forces of nature, where massive tidewater glaciers sculpt the landscape and showcase the ever-changing dance between ice and sea.

This UNESCO World Heritage Site offers a front-row seat to witness the dramatic process of glacial calving and experience the raw beauty of a world shaped by ice.

The Unique Features of Tidewater Glaciers
Tidewater glaciers are a special type of glacier that flows directly into the ocean. They are born high in the mountains, where snow accumulates and compresses into ice over centuries.

The immense weight of the ice causes the glacier to slowly creep downhill, eventually reaching the coastline.

- **Immense Scale:** Tidewater glaciers are known for their colossal size. Some, like the Margerie Glacier in Glacier Bay, can tower over 200 feet above the waterline, with even more ice hidden beneath the surface.
- **Dynamic Environment:** These glaciers are constantly changing, advancing and retreating in response to climate fluctuations. Witnessing a tidewater glacier calve – a process where large chunks of ice break off and crash into the sea – is a truly humbling experience that showcases the dynamic nature of these frozen giants.
- **Rich Ecosystems:** The interface between glacier and sea creates a unique and productive ecosystem. Nutrient-rich meltwater feeds a thriving marine environment, attracting a variety of wildlife, including humpback whales, harbor seals, and sea otters.

The Process of Calving

Calving is a natural and dramatic event that occurs when a tidewater glacier's leading edge becomes unstable and breaks off, sending massive chunks of ice plunging into the water. This process is caused by a combination of factors, including:

- **Melting:** Warmer air and water temperatures cause the glacier's leading edge to melt, weakening its structure.
- **Buoyancy:** As the glacier extends into the water, the buoyant force of the water can lift and destabilize the ice.
- **Stress and Fractures:** The constant movement of the glacier creates stress and fractures within the ice, eventually leading to calving events.

Witnessing a calving event is an exhilarating and awe-inspiring experience. The thunderous roar as the ice crashes into the water, the resulting waves, and the sight of newly formed icebergs drifting away create a powerful reminder of nature's raw power and beauty.

Exploring Glacier Bay

Due to its remote location and protected status, most visitors experience Glacier Bay National Park by cruise ship or scenic flightseeing tour.

Cruise Ships:

Multiple cruise lines offer itineraries that include a day in Glacier Bay, allowing you to witness tidewater glaciers, abundant wildlife, and stunning scenery from the comfort of a ship. Park rangers often come aboard to provide interpretive talks and answer questions about the park's natural and cultural history. Choose a smaller ship for a more intimate experience and potentially closer access to glaciers.

Scenic Flightseeing Tours:

Soar above Glacier Bay's breathtaking landscapes on a scenic flightseeing tour, offering a unique perspective of its glaciers, mountains, and fjords. Several tour operators offer a variety of flightseeing options, including helicopter tours that land on glaciers and fixed-wing flights that provide panoramic views. Flightseeing is an excellent choice for those seeking a more personalized and adventurous experience, with the added bonus of incredible aerial photography opportunities.

Inside Passage: Cruising Through Scenic Waterways

The Inside Passage, a network of sheltered waterways winding through Southeast Alaska's islands and mainland, offers a mesmerizing journey through some of the planet's most stunning scenery.

This iconic route showcases a captivating blend of picturesque towns, pristine islands, and abundant wildlife, making it a must-experience for any Alaska visitor.

Picturesque Towns and Islands:

- **Ketchikan:** Known as the "Salmon Capital of the World," this vibrant town boasts a rich cultural heritage, colorful totem poles, and opportunities for salmon fishing and bear viewing.
- **Juneau**: Alaska's capital city, Juneau, is nestled amidst a dramatic backdrop of mountains and glaciers. Explore its charming downtown, ride the Mount Roberts Tramway for panoramic views, or visit the Mendenhall Glacier.
- **Skagway:** Step back in time to the Gold Rush era in this historic town. Ride the White Pass & Yukon Route railway, hike the Chilkoot Trail, or try your hand at panning for gold.
- **Sitka:** A blend of Russian and Tlingit cultures, Sitka offers a unique historical experience. Visit St. Michael's Cathedral, the Sitka National Historical Park, or witness the majesty of bald eagles at the Alaska Raptor Center.
- **Misty Fjords National Monument:** This remote wilderness area boasts dramatic fjords, towering cliffs, and cascading waterfalls. Accessible only by boat or plane, it's a true hidden gem of the Inside Passage.

Wildlife Encounters:

- **Whales:** The Inside Passage is a prime whale-watching destination, with opportunities to spot humpback whales, orcas, and even the elusive blue whale.
- **Bears:** Keep your eyes peeled for brown bears and black bears foraging along the shoreline or fishing in streams.
- **Eagles:** Bald eagles are a common sight, soaring overhead or perched atop towering trees.
- **Sea Otters:** These playful creatures can often be seen floating on their backs, cracking open shellfish with rocks.
- **Sea Lions and Seals:** Observe these charismatic pinnipeds basking on rocky outcrops or swimming in the channels.

Choosing the Best Ferry or Cruise Itinerary:

Ferry:

- **Alaska Marine Highway System:** The state-run ferry system offers flexible itineraries and affordable fares, allowing you to explore the Inside Passage at your own pace.
- **Ideal for:** Independent travelers, budget-minded explorers, and those seeking a more immersive experience in coastal communities.

Tips:

- Book early, especially during peak season, as ferries can fill up quickly.
- Consider purchasing a multi-trip pass for greater flexibility and potential savings.
- Pack for varying weather conditions, as temperatures and precipitation can change rapidly on the water.

Cruise:

- **Variety of Cruise Lines and Itineraries:** Numerous cruise lines offer Inside Passage itineraries, ranging from large, all-inclusive ships to smaller, expedition-style vessels.
- **Ideal for:** Travelers seeking a comfortable and hassle-free experience with onboard amenities, organized excursions, and opportunities for relaxation.

Tips:

- Choose a cruise line and itinerary that aligns with your interests and budget.
- Consider a smaller ship for a more personalized experience and access to less-visited ports.
- Book shore excursions in advance, especially for popular activities.
- Research the ports of call to plan independent exploration and maximize your time ashore.

Factors to Consider When Choosing:

- **Budget:** Ferries are generally more affordable than cruises, but consider the added costs of accommodations and meals when traveling by ferry.
- **Time:** Cruises typically offer shorter itineraries with less flexibility, while ferries allow you to customize your journey and spend more time in each port.
- **Interests:** If wildlife viewing and scenic beauty are your priorities, a smaller cruise or ferry with ample outdoor space might be ideal. If you prefer a more structured and all-inclusive experience, a larger cruise ship could be the better choice.
- **Travel Style:** Independent travelers might enjoy the freedom of ferry travel, while those seeking a more relaxed and pampered experience might prefer a cruise.

Whether you opt for the flexibility of a ferry or the comforts of a cruise, exploring the Inside Passage will undoubtedly be a highlight of your Alaskan adventure. With its captivating blend of natural beauty, cultural richness, and wildlife encounters, this iconic waterway offers an unforgettable journey through the heart of the Last Frontier.

Other Must-See Natural Attractions: Waterfalls, Hot Springs, and More

While Alaska is renowned for its majestic glaciers and towering mountains, the state boasts a wealth of other natural wonders that will leave you equally awestruck.

From cascading waterfalls and soothing hot springs to volcanic landscapes and pristine lakes, these hidden gems deserve a spot on your Alaskan itinerary:

Waterfalls:
- **Mendenhall Glacier and Nugget Falls:** Located near Juneau, this iconic glacier and its accompanying waterfall create a breathtaking spectacle. Hike the trails, kayak in Mendenhall Lake, or take a guided tour to experience their grandeur.
- **Brooks Falls:** In Katmai National Park, witness the thrilling sight of brown bears fishing for salmon at Brooks Falls. Access the falls via a scenic floatplane trip or a guided bear-viewing tour.
- **Thunderbird Falls:** Near Anchorage, this easily accessible waterfall offers a refreshing escape into nature. Enjoy a short hike through the forest to reach the falls and admire their cascading beauty.

Hot Springs:
- **Chena Hot Springs Resort**: Located near Fairbanks, this resort boasts natural hot springs, an ice museum, and prime Northern Lights viewing opportunities. Soak in the warm mineral waters, surrounded by snowy landscapes, for a truly rejuvenating experience.
- **Manley Hot Springs:** Reachable by boat or small plane, this remote hot springs offers a rustic and secluded retreat. Enjoy a soak in the natural pools while surrounded by pristine wilderness.

Volcanic Landscapes:

- **Katmai National Park and Preserve:** Home to the Valley of Ten Thousand Smokes, a vast volcanic landscape formed by the 1912 eruption of Novarupta Volcano. Explore this otherworldly terrain on a guided tour or hike, marveling at the steaming fumaroles and colorful volcanic deposits.
- **Lake Clark National Park and Preserve:** Witness the active volcanoes of the Alaska Peninsula, including Mount Redoubt and Mount Iliamna. Take a scenic flightseeing tour or embark on a backcountry adventure to experience the raw power of these volcanic giants.

Pristine Lakes:

- **Kenai Lake:** This picturesque lake near Seward offers opportunities for boating, kayaking, fishing, and hiking along its scenic shoreline.
- **Wonder Lake:** Nestled in Denali National Park, Wonder Lake provides stunning views of Mount Denali reflected in its clear waters. Enjoy a leisurely stroll along the lakeshore or embark on a scenic boat tour.

Accessing and Enjoying these Attractions:

- **Transportation:** Depending on the location, these attractions may be accessible by road, boat, small plane, or a combination of transportation methods. Research transportation options in advance and book tours or rentals as needed.
- **Guided Tours:** Consider joining a guided tour for expert insights, convenient transportation, and access to remote areas. Many tour operators offer specialized excursions focusing on specific attractions, such as bear viewing, waterfall hikes, or volcanic exploration.
- **Self-Guided Exploration:** For more adventurous travelers, self-guided exploration is possible for some attractions. Be sure to research trail conditions, weather forecasts, and safety precautions before venturing out on your own.
- **Permits and Reservations:** Some attractions, particularly in national parks, may require permits or advanced reservations. Check with park authorities or tour operators to ensure you have the necessary access.

- **Seasonal Considerations:** Accessibility and weather conditions can vary throughout the year. Some attractions may be closed or have limited access during winter months. Research seasonal information and plan accordingly.

Remember:
- **Pack appropriately**: Dress in layers, wear comfortable footwear, and bring rain gear, even in summer.
- **Respect nature:** Stay on designated trails, avoid disturbing wildlife, and leave no trace.
- **Be prepared:** Check weather forecasts, carry essentials like water and snacks, and let someone know your itinerary.

By venturing beyond the well-trodden paths and exploring these hidden natural wonders, you'll discover the true diversity and beauty of Alaska's landscapes. These unforgettable experiences will add depth and richness to your Alaskan adventure, creating memories that will last a lifetime.

CHAPTER 3

Experiencing Alaskan Culture and History

A laska's wild beauty isn't just about scenery. It's about the people who've lived here for centuries. Let's dive into their stories.

Alaska Native Heritage: Rich Traditions and Modern Expression

Alaska's indigenous peoples, representing a heritage of diverse cultures and languages, have thrived in this challenging environment for millennia.

Their deep connection to the land, their rich traditions, and their enduring spirit have shaped the very essence of Alaska. To truly understand and appreciate the Last Frontier, it's essential to delve into the vibrant world of Alaska Native heritage.

Diverse Cultures and Traditions:
Alaska is home to over 20 distinct Alaska Native cultures, each with its own unique language, art forms, and way of life. These cultures can be broadly grouped into five major regions:

- **Arctic:** The Iñupiat and St. Lawrence Island Yupik peoples inhabit the northernmost reaches of Alaska, adapting to the harsh Arctic environment through resourceful hunting and fishing practices.
- **Interior:** Athabascan groups, such as the Koyukon, Gwich'in, and Tanana, thrive in the Interior region's vast forests and river valleys, relying on caribou, moose, and salmon for sustenance.
- **Southcentral:** The Dena'ina and Ahtna people call Southcentral Alaska home, navigating its diverse landscapes, from mountains and glaciers to coastal plains.
- **Southwest:** The Yup'ik, Cup'ik, and Alutiiq peoples inhabit the coastal regions of Southwest Alaska, relying on the bounty of the sea for their livelihoods.
- **Southeast:** The Tlingit, Haida, and Tsimshian peoples dominate Southeast Alaska's Inside Passage, known for their intricate totem poles, ceremonial regalia, and skilled craftsmanship.

These diverse cultures share a deep respect for the natural world, a strong sense of community, and a rich oral tradition that has been passed down through generations.

Museums, Cultural Centers, and Events to Explore:
- **Alaska Native Heritage Center (Anchorage):** This immersive cultural center showcases the traditions and contemporary arts of Alaska's 11 major cultural groups. Explore traditional dwellings, witness captivating dance performances, and interact with knowledgeable cultural interpreters.
- **Sealaska Heritage Institute (Juneau):** Dedicated to preserving and promoting Southeast Alaska's Tlingit, Haida, and Tsimshian cultures, this institute offers exhibits, workshops, and events celebrating their rich artistic heritage.
- **Totem Heritage Center (Ketchikan):** Explore the world of totem poles, learning about their symbolism and cultural significance. Admire the collection of restored totem poles and witness carvers at work.

- **Inupiat Heritage Center (Barrow)**: Discover the unique culture and history of the Iñupiat people through exhibits, demonstrations, and interactive programs. Learn about their traditional subsistence practices and their adaptations to the Arctic environment.
- **World Eskimo-Indian Olympics (Fairbanks):** Witness the athletic prowess and cultural pride of Alaska Native athletes during this annual event, featuring traditional games like the high kick, blanket toss, and seal hop.
- **Celebration (Juneau):** Immerse yourself in Southeast Alaska's vibrant Native cultures during this biennial festival, showcasing traditional dance, music, storytelling, and arts and crafts.

Additional Tips for Experiencing Alaska Native Culture:

- **Visit local villages:** Venture beyond the major cities and explore smaller communities where you can interact with Alaska Native residents, learn about their daily lives, and witness their cultural practices firsthand.
- **Attend cultural events:** Seek out local events and festivals celebrating Alaska Native heritage, such as potlatches, dance performances, and storytelling gatherings.

- **Support Alaska Native artists and businesses:** Purchase authentic arts and crafts directly from local artisans, contributing to the preservation and continuation of their cultural traditions.
- **Engage in respectful dialogue:** Show genuine interest in learning about Alaska Native cultures and traditions. Ask questions, listen attentively, and be mindful of cultural sensitivities.

By immersing yourself in the vibrant world of Alaska Native heritage, you'll gain a deeper appreciation for the rich heritage of cultures that have shaped the Last Frontier.Embrace the opportunity to learn, connect, and celebrate the enduring spirit of Alaska's indigenous peoples.

Gold Rush History: Relive the Klondike Era

The Klondike Gold Rush, a frenzy of fortune-seekers driven by dreams of striking it rich, forever etched its mark on Alaska's history. This late 19th-century stampede transformed sleepy towns into bustling boomtowns, drawing thousands of prospectors to the unforgiving wilderness in search of glittering gold. Relive the excitement and hardships of this extraordinary era by exploring these historic sites, museums, and tours that bring the Gold Rush to life:

Skagway: Gateway to the Gold Fields

- **Klondike Gold Rush National Historical Park:** This park preserves the heart of Skagway's gold rush heritage. Stroll along Broadway Street, lined with restored buildings and wooden sidewalks, or hike the Chilkoot Trail, a challenging route that tested the mettle of countless stampeders.
- **White Pass & Yukon Route Railway:** Embark on a scenic train journey aboard this historic narrow-gauge railway, retracing the footsteps of prospectors as you climb through breathtaking mountain passes and witness cascading waterfalls.
- **Red Onion Saloon Museum:** Once a notorious brothel during the Gold Rush, this museum offers a glimpse into the bawdy and colorful side of Skagway's past.

Dawson City: Heart of the Klondike

- **Dawson City:** Designated a National Historic Site, Dawson City retains much of its Gold Rush-era charm. Wander its dirt streets, visit historic buildings like the Palace Grand Theatre and Robert Service Cabin, and try your luck at panning for gold in the Klondike River.
- **Dredge No. 4:** This massive gold dredge, a testament to the industrial scale of mining operations, offers a fascinating glimpse into the technology and techniques used during the Gold Rush.
- **Jack London Museum:** Dedicated to the renowned author who spent time in the Klondike, this museum showcases his life and works, offering insights into the hardships and triumphs of the Gold Rush era.

Other Historic Sites & Tours

- **Independence Mine State Historical Park (Hatcher Pass):** Explore the remnants of a once-thriving gold mine, including the mill building, bunkhouses, and mine shafts. Take a guided tour or hike the scenic trails for panoramic views of the surrounding mountains.
- **Kennecott Mines National Historic Landmark:** Located in Wrangell-St. Elias National Park, this abandoned copper mining town offers a haunting glimpse into the boom-and-bust cycle of resource extraction.

- **Gold Rush-themed tours:** Several tour operators offer guided excursions that delve deeper into the history and legacy of the Klondike Gold Rush, including visits to historic sites, gold panning demonstrations, and storytelling sessions that bring the era to life.

Experiencing the Gold Rush Legacy
- **Pan for Gold:** Try your hand at panning for gold in the Klondike or other historic gold-bearing streams. Several outfitters offer guided tours and equipment rentals.
- **Attend a Gold Rush-themed event:** Experience the spirit of the Gold Rush by participating in events like the annual Skagway Days festival or the Dawson City Music Festival.
- **Explore Gold Rush literature and films:** Immerse yourself in the stories of the Klondike through classic works like Jack London's "Call of the Wild" or Charlie Chaplin's film "The Gold Rush."

The Klondike Gold Rush may be a chapter of history, but its legacy lives on in the towns, trails, and stories that shaped Alaska's identity. By exploring these historic sites and engaging with the Gold Rush's cultural remnants, you'll gain a deeper appreciation for the courage, resilience, and ambition that defined this extraordinary era.

Museums and Cultural Centers: Explore the Alaskan Life

Alaska's museums and cultural centers offer fascinating glimpses into the state's diverse heritage, artistic expressions, and natural wonders. Here's a curated selection of must-visit institutions that will enrich your understanding of the Last Frontier:

Anchorage Museum

- **Highlights:** As Alaska's largest museum, it houses an extensive collection of Alaskan art, artifacts, and natural history exhibits. Explore the Smithsonian Arctic Studies Center, marvel at contemporary Alaskan artworks, and engage with interactive science exhibits.

Practical Information:

- **Location:** Anchorage
- **Hours:** Vary seasonally, typically open daily
- **Admission:** Fees apply, with discounts for seniors, students, and military personnel. Check the website for current rates and special exhibitions.

Alaska Wildlife Conservation Center

- **Highlights:** Encounter rescued and rehabilitated Alaskan animals, including bears, moose, wolves, and eagles, in spacious natural habitats. Drive or take a guided tour through the center to learn about these magnificent creatures and their conservation stories.

Practical Information:

- **Location**: Near Portage, about an hour's drive from Anchorage
- **Hours**: Open daily, year-round

- **Admission:** Fees apply, with discounts for children and seniors. Check the website for current rates and special events.

Totem Heritage Center (Ketchikan)

- **Highlights:** Explore the world of Tlingit and Haida totem poles, learning about their symbolism, cultural significance, and artistic techniques. Admire the collection of restored totem poles and witness carvers at work.

Practical Information:

- **Location:** Ketchikan
- **Hours:** Vary seasonally, typically open daily
- **Admission:** Free admission

Sheldon Museum and Cultural Center (Haines)

- **Highlights:** Explore the rich cultural heritage of the Chilkat Tlingit people through exhibits showcasing their traditional art, artifacts, and history. Learn about their weaving techniques, ceremonial practices, and connection to the land.

Practical Information:
- **Location:** Haines
- **Hours:** Vary seasonally, typically open Tuesday through Saturday
- **Admission:** Fees apply, with discounts for seniors and students. Check the website for current rates and special exhibits.

University of Alaska Museum of the North (Fairbanks)
- **Highlights:** Discover the natural and cultural history of Alaska through a vast collection of exhibits, including dinosaur fossils, Alaska Native artifacts, and contemporary art. Experience the aurora borealis in the museum's planetarium.

Practical Information:
- **Location:** Fairbanks
- **Hours:** Vary seasonally, typically open daily
- **Admission:** Fees apply, with discounts for seniors, students, and military personnel. Check the website for current rates and special events.

Remember:
Check museum websites for the most up-to-date information on hours, admission fees, and special exhibits. Consider purchasing a membership if you plan to visit multiple museums during your trip. Allow ample time to explore each museum and appreciate its unique offerings. Engage with knowledgeable staff and volunteers to enhance your understanding of the exhibits and Alaska's rich cultural heritage.

By visiting these and other museums and cultural centers, you'll gain a deeper appreciation for Alaska's history, art, and natural wonders. These institutions offer a window into the soul of the Last Frontier, enriching your journey and leaving a lasting impression.

Festivals and Events: Celebrate with the Locals

Throughout the year, Alaska comes alive with a vibrant heritage of festivals and events that celebrate its unique culture, heritage, and natural wonders. Immerse yourself in the local festivities, witness traditional performances, and savor the flavors of Alaska's culinary scene.

Here's a glimpse into some of the annual events that showcase the state's vibrant spirit:

Winter:
- **Fur Rendezvous Festival (Anchorage, February):** This iconic winter carnival features a thrilling mix of outdoor activities, cultural events, and quirky competitions, including the Running of the Reindeer and the Outhouse Races.
- **Iditarod Trail Sled Dog Race (Anchorage to Nome, March):** Witness the world-famous dog sled race as mushers and their teams embark on a grueling 1,000-mile journey across Alaska's rugged terrain.
- **World Ice Art Championships (Fairbanks, February-March):** Marvel at the intricate ice sculptures created by artists from around the world during this dazzling competition.

Spring:
- **Alaska Folk Festival (Juneau, April):** Enjoy a week-long celebration of folk music, featuring talented musicians from across Alaska and beyond.
- **Kodiak Crab Festival (Kodiak, May):** Indulge in the freshest seafood and celebrate the island's fishing heritage during this lively festival.

Summer:

- **Golden Days Celebration (Fairbanks, July):** Commemorate the anniversary of the discovery of gold in Fairbanks with parades, live music, and family-friendly activities.

- **Alaska State Fair (Palmer, August-September):** Experience the state's largest agricultural fair, showcasing giant vegetables, livestock competitions, live entertainment, and delicious food.

- **Salmonfest (Ninilchik, August):** Celebrate Alaska's iconic salmon with live music, food vendors, and educational activities highlighting sustainable fishing practices.

Fall:

- **Alaska Day Festival (Sitka, October):** Commemorate the transfer of Alaska from Russia to the United States with parades, historical reenactments, and cultural events.

- **Oktoberfest (Anchorage and Fairbanks, September-October):** Join the Bavarian-inspired festivities with traditional food, music, and beer gardens.

Year-Round:

- **First Friday Art Walks (Various locations):** Explore local art galleries and studios during these monthly events, offering a glimpse into Alaska's vibrant arts scene.
- **Native cultural events and performances:** Throughout the year, communities across Alaska host events showcasing traditional dance, music, storytelling, and arts and crafts. Check local listings for specific dates and locations.

Beyond the Calendar:

- **Embrace spontaneity:** While these annual events offer a glimpse into Alaskan culture, don't hesitate to embrace the unexpected. Strike up conversations with locals, attend community gatherings, and immerse yourself in the everyday rhythms of Alaskan life.
- **Seek out hidden gems:** Explore local markets, attend art exhibitions, and discover off-the-beaten-path events that showcase the unique character of each community you visit.

By participating in these festivals and events, you'll not only witness the vibrant spirit of Alaska but also create lasting connections with the people and cultures that make this state so special.

CHAPTER 4

Alaskan Adventures for Every Traveler

Hiking boots? Check. Kayak paddle? Check. Sense of adventure? Double check. It's time to get out there and experience Alaska!

Wildlife Viewing: Spotting Bears, Whales, and More

Alaska's untamed wilderness teems with iconic wildlife, offering unparalleled opportunities to witness these magnificent creatures in their natural habitat.

From majestic brown bears fishing for salmon to graceful humpback whales breaching in icy waters, Alaska's wildlife encounters are sure to leave a lasting impression.

Tips on Spotting Wildlife:
- **Timing is Key:** Early mornings and evenings are prime times for wildlife activity. Animals are often more active during these cooler hours, seeking food and water.

- **Patience is a Virtue:** Wildlife viewing requires patience and observation. Take your time, scan the landscape, and listen for sounds of movement.
- **Use Binoculars and a Camera with a Zoom Lens:** These tools will enhance your viewing experience and allow you to capture close-up photos of wildlife from a safe distance.
- **Respect Wildlife:** Maintain a safe distance from animals and never approach or feed them. Follow park regulations and guidelines to ensure both your safety and the well-being of the wildlife.
- **Hire a Guide:** Consider joining a guided wildlife tour for expert insights, increased chances of spotting elusive creatures, and a safe and educational experience.

Recommended Guided Tours, Wildlife Cruises, and National Parks:

Bears:
- **Katmai National Park:** Renowned for its brown bear population, particularly at Brooks Falls during the salmon run. Guided bear-viewing tours offer safe and unforgettable encounters.
- **Anan Creek Wildlife Observatory:** Witness black bears and bald eagles feasting on salmon at this popular viewing site near Wrangell. Guided tours are available during peak season.

Whales:
- **Kenai Fjords National Park:** Embark on a whale-watching cruise from Seward to witness humpback whales, orcas, and other marine life in their natural habitat.
- **Juneau:** The waters around Juneau are teeming with humpback whales during the summer months. Join a whale-watching tour for a chance to see these majestic creatures up close.

Moose:
- **Denali National Park:** Moose are frequently spotted along the Denali Park Road, especially in the early morning or evening hours. Bus tours offer excellent opportunities for moose viewing.

- **Chugach State Park:** Located near Anchorage, this vast park provides habitat for moose, bears, and other wildlife. Hike the trails or drive the scenic roads for a chance to encounter these creatures.

Eagles:
- **Chilkat Bald Eagle Preserve:** Near Haines, this preserve is home to the world's largest concentration of bald eagles during the salmon run in fall. Guided tours and viewing platforms offer excellent vantage points.
- **Klawock:** Known as the "City of Eagles," this Tlingit village on Prince of Wales Island boasts a large population of bald eagles. Take a guided tour or explore on your own to witness these majestic birds in their natural habitat.

Other Iconic Alaskan Animals:
- **Dall Sheep:** These agile mountain dwellers can be spotted in Denali National Park, Wrangell-St. Elias National Park, and other mountainous regions.
- **Caribou:** Vast herds of caribou roam the Arctic National Wildlife Refuge and other areas of Alaska's Interior. Guided tours or scenic flights offer the best opportunities for viewing.

- **Wolves:** While elusive, wolves can sometimes be seen in Denali National Park and other remote areas. Join a guided wolf-watching tour for a chance to hear their haunting howls and catch a glimpse of these apex predators.

Remember:
Research and choose reputable tour operators who prioritize ethical wildlife viewing practices and the safety of both animals and visitors. Pack binoculars, a camera with a zoom lens, and appropriate clothing for outdoor adventures. Be patient, observant, and respectful of wildlife. Your reward will be unforgettable encounters with some of the planet's most magnificent creatures.

By following these tips and exploring the recommended destinations, you'll increase your chances of witnessing Alaska's diverse and captivating wildlife. These encounters will undoubtedly be a highlight of your trip, creating lasting memories and a deeper appreciation for the delicate balance of nature in the Last Frontier.

Hiking and Backpacking: Trails for All Levels

Alaska's vast and diverse landscapes offer a hiker's paradise, with trails ranging from leisurely strolls through lush rainforests to challenging multi-day treks across glaciers and mountain passes.

Easy Walks:

Exit Glacier Trail (Kenai Fjords National Park):
This accessible trail winds through a lush forest, offering stunning views of the receding Exit Glacier and the surrounding mountains. Perfect for families and those seeking a gentle introduction to Alaska's wilderness.

- **Winner Creek Trail (Girdwood):** This scenic trail meanders along a rushing creek, passing through forests and meadows. Highlights include a hand tram across a gorge and opportunities for wildlife viewing.
- **Tongass National Forest Trails (Southeast Alaska):** The Tongass, the largest national forest in the US, offers numerous short and easy trails, perfect for experiencing the region's unique temperate rainforest ecosystem.

Moderate Hikes:
- **Harding Icefield Trail (Kenai Fjords National Park):** This challenging but rewarding trail climbs steeply to the edge of the Harding Icefield, offering panoramic views of glaciers, mountains, and the vast expanse of ice.
- **Mount Roberts Trail (Juneau):** Ascend through lush rainforest to the summit of Mount Roberts for breathtaking views of Juneau, the Gastineau Channel, and surrounding mountains.

- **Reed Lakes Trail (Hatcher Pass):** This scenic trail winds through alpine meadows and past turquoise lakes, offering stunning vistas of the Talkeetna Mountains.

Challenging Treks:
- **Chilkoot Trail (Skagway):** Retrace the footsteps of gold rush stampeders on this historic 33-mile trail, crossing the Coast Mountains and offering a glimpse into the challenges and triumphs of this bygone era.
- **Kesugi Ridge Trail (Denali State Park):** This strenuous 29-mile trail traverses a scenic ridgeline, offering breathtaking views of Denali and the Alaska Range.
- **Gates of the Arctic National Park**: This vast and remote park offers endless opportunities for backcountry exploration and challenging treks through untouched wilderness.

Essential Safety Tips for Hiking in Bear Country:
- **Make Noise:** Talk, sing, or clap your hands periodically to alert bears to your presence and avoid surprising them.
- **Travel in Groups:** There's safety in numbers. Hiking with others reduces the risk of bear encounters.
- **Carry Bear Spray:** Bear spray is an effective deterrent in case of a close encounter. Know how to use it properly and keep it readily accessible.
- **Store Food Properly:** Use bear-resistant canisters or hang food bags at least 10 feet off the ground and 4 feet away from tree trunks.
- **Be Aware of Your Surroundings:** Watch for signs of bear activity, such as tracks, scat, or diggings. Avoid hiking at dawn or dusk, when bears are most active.

Navigating Alaska's Rugged Terrain:
- **Plan Ahead**: Research trail conditions, weather forecasts, and potential hazards before embarking on any hike.
- **Pack Essentials:** Carry a map, compass, first-aid kit, extra food and water, and appropriate clothing for changing weather conditions.
- **Inform Others**: Let someone know your itinerary and expected return time.

- **Be Prepared for Wildlife Encounters:** Carry bear spray and know how to use it. Maintain a safe distance from all wildlife.
- **Respect the Environment:** Stay on designated trails, leave no trace, and practice responsible outdoor ethics.

Remember, Alaska's wilderness is both beautiful and unpredictable. By following these safety tips and being prepared for the challenges of the terrain, you can enjoy a safe and rewarding hiking or backpacking adventure in the Last Frontier.

Kayaking and Canoeing: Paddle Through Pristine Waters

Alaska's pristine waterways offer an unparalleled playground for kayakers and canoeists of all levels. From tranquil lakes reflecting majestic mountains to protected bays teeming with marine life, paddling through Alaska's stunning scenery is an unforgettable experience.

Picturesque Waterways:

Kachemak Bay (Homer):
This expansive bay offers sheltered waters, diverse wildlife, and stunning views of glaciers and mountains. Paddle among sea otters, seals, and seabirds while enjoying the tranquil beauty of this scenic area.

- **Resurrection Bay (Seward):** Explore the dramatic fjords and glaciers of Resurrection Bay, home to abundant marine life and breathtaking scenery. Guided tours offer access to secluded coves and opportunities for wildlife encounters.
- **Mendenhall Lake (Juneau):** Paddle across this glacier-fed lake, surrounded by towering peaks and the awe-inspiring Mendenhall Glacier. Witness icebergs drifting in the water and listen for the thunderous roar of calving ice.

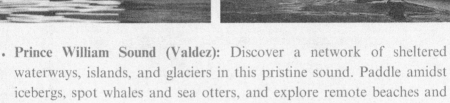

- **Prince William Sound (Valdez):** Discover a network of sheltered waterways, islands, and glaciers in this pristine sound. Paddle amidst icebergs, spot whales and sea otters, and explore remote beaches and coves.
- **Inside Passage (Southeast Alaska):** The sheltered waters of the Inside Passage offer countless opportunities for kayaking and canoeing, with options ranging from day trips to multi-day expeditions. Explore hidden coves, visit remote islands, and witness diverse wildlife.

Guided Tours for All Abilities:
- **Beginner:** For those new to paddling, consider a guided tour on calm waters with experienced guides who provide instruction and support.
- **Intermediate:** Experienced paddlers can choose tours with longer distances, more challenging conditions, or opportunities for camping and wilderness exploration.
- **Advanced:** Seek out multi-day expeditions or guided trips to remote areas for a true Alaskan wilderness adventure.

Safety Tips:
- **Dress for the Water:** Wear a wetsuit or drysuit, even in summer, as water temperatures can be cold.

- **Wear a Life Jacket:** Always wear a properly fitted life jacket, regardless of your swimming ability.
- **Paddle with a Partner:** Never paddle alone. It's safer and more enjoyable to share the experience.
- **Check Weather and Tides**: Be aware of changing weather conditions and tidal currents, especially in open waters.
- **File a Float Plan:** Let someone know your itinerary and expected return time.

Kayaking Gear and Rentals:
- **Kayak and Paddle:** Choose a kayak appropriate for your skill level and the type of paddling you plan to do. Rentals are available in many towns and cities.
- **Life Jacket:** A properly fitted life jacket is essential for safety.
- **Spray Skirt**: A spray skirt helps keep water out of your kayak, especially in rough conditions.
- **Dry Bags:** Protect your gear from water damage with dry bags.
- **Paddle Float and Bilge Pump:** These safety tools can help you recover from a capsize.

Recommendations:
- **Kenai Fjords Glacier Lodge:** Offers guided kayaking tours in Aialik Bay, showcasing stunning glaciers and marine life.
- **Liquid Adventures (Juneau):** Provides a variety of kayaking tours in Mendenhall Lake and the surrounding areas.
- **Alaska Sea Kayakers (Whittier):** Specializes in multi-day kayaking expeditions in Prince William Sound.
- **Spirit Walker Expeditions (Sitka):** Offers guided kayaking tours and expeditions in the breathtaking waters of Southeast Alaska.

Embrace the tranquility and adventure of paddling through Alaska's waterways. With its picturesque scenery and abundant wildlife, kayaking and canoeing offer an unforgettable way to experience the Last Frontier's natural wonders.

Fishing: Reel in Salmon, Halibut, and Trout

Alaska's pristine waters teem with a rich diversity of fish, offering unparalleled opportunities for anglers of all levels. Whether you're casting a line in a remote stream, fly fishing in a crystal-clear river, or reeling in a trophy-sized halibut from the depths of the ocean, Alaska's fishing experiences are sure to create memories that last a lifetime.

Types of Fishing in Alaska:

Freshwater Fishing:

- **Salmon:** The iconic Alaskan salmon, with its five species (King, Sockeye, Coho, Pink, and Chum), draws anglers from around the world. Cast your line in rivers, streams, and lakes for a chance to catch these prized fish during their annual runs.
- **Trout:** Alaska's rivers and lakes boast healthy populations of Rainbow Trout, Dolly Varden, Lake Trout, and Arctic Grayling, offering exciting opportunities for fly fishing and spin fishing.
- **Northern Pike**: These ferocious predators lurk in the shallow waters of lakes and rivers, providing a thrilling challenge for anglers seeking a trophy catch.

Saltwater Fishing:

- **Halibut:** The mighty halibut, one of the largest flatfish in the world, draws anglers to Alaska's coastal waters for a chance to reel in a record-breaking catch.
- **Rockfish**: These abundant and colorful fish offer a delicious and accessible target for saltwater anglers of all skill levels.
- **Lingcod:** These fierce predators inhabit rocky reefs and kelp forests, providing a challenging and rewarding fishing experience.

Fly Fishing:

Alaska's pristine rivers and streams offer world-class fly fishing opportunities, with experienced guides leading anglers to prime spots for salmon, trout, and other species. Consider a float trip down a scenic river for a truly immersive fly fishing experience.

Fishing Licenses and Regulations:

- **Non-Resident Fishing License:** Required for all non-residents 16 years and older. Purchase online or at local sporting goods stores.
- **King Salmon Stamp:** An additional stamp is required to fish for King Salmon.
- **Regulations:** Familiarize yourself with the specific regulations for the species and location you plan to fish, including bag limits, size restrictions, and seasonal closures.
- **Catch and Release:** Consider practicing catch and release to help preserve fish populations for future generations.

Recommended Fishing Charters:

- **Kenai River:** The Kenai River is world-renowned for its salmon and trout fishing. Numerous charters operate from towns like Soldotna and Kenai, offering guided trips for all skill levels.
- **Seward**: Explore the rich fishing grounds of Resurrection Bay with a charter boat from Seward. Target halibut, salmon, rockfish, and other species while enjoying stunning scenery.
- **Ketchikan:** Join a saltwater charter from Ketchikan to fish for salmon, halibut, and other species in the productive waters of the Inside Passage.
- **Kodiak:** Experience world-class fishing for halibut, salmon, and rockfish in the remote waters around Kodiak Island. Fly-in lodges and fishing charters offer unforgettable experiences.

Remember:

- **Choose a Reputable Operator:** Research and select a licensed and experienced fishing charter or guide service with a good safety record.
- **Pack Appropriately:** Dress in layers and bring rain gear, as weather conditions can change quickly on the water.

- **Respect the Resource:** Follow all fishing regulations and practice ethical fishing practices to ensure the sustainability of Alaska's fisheries.

Fishing in Alaska is an adventure in itself, offering not only the thrill of the catch but also the chance to immerse yourself in the state's pristine wilderness and witness its abundant wildlife. Whether you're a seasoned angler or a novice, casting a line in Alaska's waters is an experience that will leave you hooked.

Dog Sledding and Snowmobiling: Winter Thrillslibut, and Trout

When the snow blankets Alaska's landscapes, a world of thrilling winter adventures awaits. Feel the rush of gliding across frozen trails, surrounded by pristine wilderness and breathtaking scenery.

Whether you choose the traditional charm of dog sledding or the adrenaline-pumping excitement of snowmobiling, you're sure to create unforgettable memories in Alaska's winter wonderland.

Dog Sledding: A Timeless Alaskan Tradition
- **Mush through the wilderness:** Experience the thrill of mushing your own team of eager huskies through snow-covered forests and frozen lakes. Feel the connection with these incredible animals and the power of their teamwork as you glide across the winter landscape.
- **Kennel visits and meet-and-greets:** Get up close and personal with the dogs, learn about their training and care, and even cuddle some adorable puppies.
- **Multi-day expeditions:** Embark on a multi-day dog sledding adventure for a truly immersive experience in the Alaskan wilderness. Spend nights in cozy cabins or under the starry sky, surrounded by the serenity of the winter landscape.

Snowmobiling: Explore at Your Own Pace

- **Zoom through the backcountry**: Experience the adrenaline rush of snowmobiling across vast expanses of snow-covered terrain, accessing remote areas and enjoying breathtaking views.
- **Tailor your adventure:** Choose from a variety of snowmobile tours, ranging from gentle rides through scenic valleys to exhilarating climbs up mountain slopes.
- **Combine with other activities:** Many tour operators offer combination packages that pair snowmobiling with other winter activities like ice fishing, dog sledding, or Northern Lights viewing.

Recommended Tour Operators:
Dog Sledding:

- **Salmon Berry Tours (Seward):** Offers year-round dog sledding tours, including kennel visits, glacier dog sledding, and multi-day expeditions.
- **Seavey's IdidaRide Sled Dog Tours (Seward)**: Experience dog sledding with Iditarod champions and their team of huskies, offering tours on a glacier or through scenic valleys.
- **Snowhook Adventure Guides of Alaska (Willow):** Provides a range of dog sledding experiences, including tours with Iditarod mushers and overnight trips to remote cabins.

Snowmobiling:

- **Alaska Backcountry Adventures (Girdwood):** Explore the Chugach Mountains on guided snowmobile tours tailored to different skill levels.

- **Hatcher Pass Snowmobile Tours (Palmer):** Experience the thrill of snowmobiling through scenic Hatcher Pass, with options for both day trips and overnight adventures.

- **Northern Alaska Tour Company (Fairbanks):** Discover the vast wilderness of Alaska's Interior on guided snowmobile tours, including opportunities for Northern Lights viewing and ice fishing.

Tips for Choosing the Right Experience:

- **Skill Level:** Consider your experience level with winter activities. Dog sledding tours often require less physical exertion than snowmobiling, making them a good choice for beginners.

- **Interests:** If you're passionate about animals and crave a more traditional experience, dog sledding might be the perfect fit. If you prefer a faster-paced adventure and the freedom to explore independently, snowmobiling could be the ideal option.

- **Duration:** Tours range from short excursions to multi-day expeditions. Choose a duration that fits your schedule and desired level of immersion in the Alaskan wilderness.

- **Group Size:** Some tours offer private experiences, while others cater to larger groups. Consider your preference for a more intimate or social setting.
- **Tour Operator:** Research different tour operators and read reviews to ensure they have a good safety record, experienced guides, and well-maintained equipment.

Embrace the winter wonderland of Alaska and create unforgettable memories with a dog sledding or snowmobiling adventure. Feel the thrill of gliding across the snow, surrounded by breathtaking scenery and the magic of the Alaskan wilderness.

Northern Lights Viewing: Witness the Aurora Borealis

The aurora borealis, also known as the Northern Lights, is a breathtaking natural phenomenon that paints the night sky with vibrant colors. This mesmerizing display of dancing lights is a bucket-list experience for many travelers, and Alaska offers some of the best viewing opportunities on Earth.

The Science Behind the Aurora Borealis:
The aurora borealis is caused by collisions between charged particles from the sun and the Earth's atmosphere. When these particles collide with atoms and molecules in the atmosphere, they excite them, causing them to release energy in the form of light. The colors of the aurora depend on the type of atom or molecule that is excited, with green and red being the most common colors.

Best Times and Places to See the Northern Lights:
- **Time of Year:** The aurora borealis is most visible during the equinox months (September and March) and winter (October-April). During these periods, the nights are longer and darker, increasing the chances of seeing the lights.

- **Location:** Alaska's Interior and Arctic regions offer the best opportunities for viewing the aurora borealis due to their clear skies and minimal light pollution. Fairbanks, known as the "Aurora Capital of Alaska," boasts over 240 nights of aurora activity per year.
- **Weather Conditions:** Clear skies are essential for optimal viewing. Check weather forecasts and choose a location with minimal cloud cover.
- **Solar Activity:** The intensity of the aurora borealis depends on solar activity. Monitor space weather forecasts for predictions of heightened solar activity, which can lead to more spectacular displays.

Tips on Photographing the Northern Lights:
- **Use a Tripod:** A sturdy tripod is essential for capturing sharp images of the aurora, as long exposures are required.
- **Use a Wide-Angle Lens:** A wide-angle lens will capture more of the sky and the surrounding landscape.
- **Set a High ISO:** A high ISO setting (typically 800-3200) will allow you to capture more light in low-light conditions.
- **Use a Long Exposure:** Experiment with exposure times between 5-20 seconds, depending on the intensity of the aurora and the desired effect.
- **Focus Manually:** Set your camera to manual focus and focus on a distant object or star to ensure sharp images.

Choosing Accommodations with Optimal Viewing Opportunities:
- **Remote Locations:** Choose accommodations away from city lights for minimal light pollution and unobstructed views of the night sky.
- **Northern Exposure:** Look for lodges or cabins with windows or decks facing north, offering prime viewing opportunities for the aurora borealis.
- **Aurora Wake-Up Calls:** Some lodges offer aurora wake-up calls, notifying guests when the lights are active.
- **Hot Tubs and Outdoor Fire Pits:** Enjoy the aurora borealis in comfort from a hot tub or while gathered around an outdoor fire pit.

Recommended Accommodations:

- **Chena Hot Springs Resort (Fairbanks):** This resort offers natural hot springs, an ice museum, and prime Northern Lights viewing opportunities.
- **Borealis Basecamp (Fairbanks):** Stay in a cozy geodesic dome with panoramic views of the night sky, perfect for witnessing the aurora borealis.
- **Tongass Rainforest Retreat (Ketchikan):** This remote lodge offers guided Northern Lights viewing tours and comfortable accommodations in a pristine wilderness setting.

Remember: Witnessing the aurora borealis is a natural phenomenon and requires patience and a bit of luck. Be prepared for cold weather, dress warmly, and enjoy the serenity of the Alaskan night sky, whether the lights appear or not. By following these tips and choosing accommodations with optimal viewing opportunities, you'll increase your chances of experiencing the magic of the Northern Lights and capturing stunning photos of this celestial dance.

Family-Friendly Activities: Fun for All Ages

Alaska's breathtaking scenery, abundant wildlife, and unique cultural experiences offer a playground for families seeking adventure and connection.

Wildlife Encounters:

- **Alaska Wildlife Conservation Center (AWCC):** Meet rescued and rehabilitated animals like bears, moose, and wolves up close. Take a scenic drive or guided tour through the center and learn about these majestic creatures.

- **Alaska Sealife Center (Seward):** Explore this marine rehabilitation center and aquarium to witness rescued sea otters, seals, and seabirds. Interactive exhibits and educational programs make learning fun for all ages.
- **Whale Watching Tours:** Embark on a thrilling whale-watching cruise from Seward or Juneau for a chance to see humpback whales, orcas, and other marine mammals in their natural habitat.

Glacier Exploration:
- **Mendenhall Glacier (Juneau):** Hike to the glacier's edge, take a guided tour through the ice caves, or kayak in Mendenhall Lake for stunning views of this majestic ice formation.
- **Exit Glacier (Kenai Fjords National Park):** Witness the power of a retreating glacier and learn about its impact on the environment. Hike the accessible trail or take a guided tour to explore the glacier's features.
- **Glacier Bay National Park:** Experience the awe-inspiring beauty of tidewater glaciers calving into the sea. Take a cruise or scenic flightseeing tour for unforgettable views and encounters with marine life.

Scenic Train and Tram Rides:

- **Alaska Railroad:** Embark on a scenic train journey through Alaska's stunning landscapes. Choose from a variety of routes and enjoy comfortable seating, dining options, and breathtaking views.
- **Alyeska Aerial Tram (Girdwood):** Ascend to the summit of Mount Alyeska for panoramic views of the surrounding mountains, glaciers, and Turnagain Arm. Enjoy hiking trails, dining options, and even ziplining at the top.

Interactive Museums and Cultural Experiences:

- **Alaska Native Heritage Center (Anchorage):** Immerse yourselves in the rich traditions and contemporary arts of Alaska's indigenous peoples. Explore traditional dwellings, witness captivating dance performances, and participate in hands-on activities.
- **Anchorage Museum:** Discover Alaska's art, history, and natural wonders through engaging exhibits and interactive displays. Kids will love the Imaginarium Discovery Center and the planetarium shows.
- **Totem Heritage Center (Ketchikan):** Explore the world of Tlingit and Haida totem poles, learning about their symbolism and cultural significance. Watch carvers at work and admire the collection of restored totem poles.

Outdoor Adventures:

- **Hiking and Camping**: Explore Alaska's vast network of trails, from easy walks to moderate hikes with stunning views. Camp under the stars and experience the serenity of the wilderness.
- **Kayaking and Canoeing:** Paddle through calm waters, surrounded by breathtaking scenery and wildlife. Guided tours cater to families and provide all necessary equipment and instruction.
- **Dog Sledding:** Experience the thrill of mushing your own team of huskies through snowy landscapes. Kennel visits and meet-and-greets offer up-close encounters with these incredible animals.

Tips for Keeping Kids Entertained and Engaged:

- **Plan a mix of activities:** Balance outdoor adventures with indoor activities, such as visiting museums or enjoying a family-friendly show.

- **Allow for downtime:** Schedule breaks for rest and relaxation, especially after long hikes or active days.
- **Pack snacks and drinks:** Keep kids fueled and hydrated throughout the day with healthy snacks and plenty of water.
- **Embrace spontaneity:** Be flexible and open to unexpected detours and discoveries. Some of the best memories are made when plans change.
- **Encourage curiosity and learning:** Engage kids in conversations about the wildlife, landscapes, and cultures they encounter. Ask questions, share stories, and foster a love for the natural world.

Alaska's wonders are best experienced together. By creating a balance of adventure, education, and relaxation, your family will cherish the memories of your Alaskan journey for years to come.

CHAPTER ⑤

Practical Tips for a Smooth Trip

A lright, let's get real for a minute. Alaska's awesome, but it's also wild. Here's how to stay safe, prepared, and have the best trip possible.

Packing List: Essentials for Every Season

Packing for Alaska requires careful consideration of the season you plan to visit and the activities you'll be enjoying. Weather conditions can change rapidly, even in summer, so layering is key.

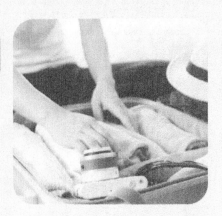

Here are detailed packing lists for each season, along with tips for packing light and efficiently:

Summer (June-August)
Clothing:
- Moisture-wicking T-shirts and long-sleeved shirts: Opt for breathable fabrics that dry quickly.
- Fleece jacket or lightweight sweater: Provides warmth for cooler evenings or hikes.

- **Waterproof jacket and pants**: Essential for rain showers, boat tours, and glacier hikes.
- **Hiking pants or shorts**: Choose comfortable, quick-drying options.
- **Swimsuit**: For dips in hot springs or lakes (if you're brave!).
- **Comfortable walking shoes or hiking boots**: Ensure good ankle support and traction.
- **Sandals or water shoes**: For relaxing at campgrounds or on the beach.
- **Hat and sunglasses**: Protect yourself from the sun, especially during long daylight hours.
- **Insect repellent**: Mosquitos can be prevalent in summer, so come prepared.

Gear:

- **Backpack**: Choose a comfortable and durable backpack for day hikes and excursions.
- **Daypack**: A smaller pack for carrying essentials like water, snacks, and a camera.
- **Water bottle**: Stay hydrated, especially during outdoor activities.
- **Sunscreen and lip balm**: Protect your skin from the sun's rays, even on cloudy days.
- **Camera and extra batteries**: Capture Alaska's stunning scenery and wildlife.
- **Binoculars**: Enhance your wildlife viewing experience.

- **Headlamp or flashlight:** For navigating campgrounds or trails after dark.
- **First-aid kit:** Be prepared for minor injuries and ailments.

Shoulder Seasons (May & September)

Follow the summer packing list, but add:

- **Warmer layers:** Include a heavier fleece jacket, thermal base layers, and warm hat and gloves.
- **Waterproof boots:** May and September can bring rain and snow, so ensure your footwear is waterproof and insulated.

Winter (October-April)

Clothing:

- **Thermal base layers:** Essential for staying warm in cold temperatures.
- **Insulated pants and jacket:** Choose waterproof and windproof options for maximum protection.
- **Warm hat, gloves, and neck gaiter:** Keep your extremities warm and covered.
- **Wool socks:** Provide warmth and moisture-wicking properties.
- **Insulated, waterproof boots:** Choose boots with good traction for walking on snow and ice.

Gear:

- **Hand and foot warmers:** Provide extra warmth during outdoor activities.
- **Ice cleats or Yaktrax:** Improve traction on icy surfaces.
- **Ski goggles or sunglasses:** Protect your eyes from glare and snow blindness.
- **Headlamp or flashlight**: Essential for navigating during short daylight hours.

Tips for Packing Light and Efficiently:

- **Layer up**: Dressing in layers allows you to adjust to changing weather conditions.
- **Choose versatile clothing:** Pack items that can be mixed and matched for multiple outfits.
- **Utilize packing cubes or compression bags:** These tools help organize your luggage and save space.
- **Roll clothes instead of folding:** Rolling helps prevent wrinkles and maximizes space.
- **Wear your bulkiest items on the plane:** Save space in your luggage by wearing your hiking boots or heavy jacket during travel.
- **Do laundry:** If you're on a longer trip, consider doing laundry at your accommodations or a laundromat to reduce the amount of clothing you need to pack.

Pack for the activities you plan to do. If you'll be hiking, bring sturdy boots; if you'll be spending time on a boat, bring waterproof gear. Check the weather forecast before you go and pack accordingly. Leave room in your luggage for souvenirs and treasures you'll find along the way. By following these packing tips and preparing for Alaska's varied weather conditions, you'll be ready to embrace any adventure that comes your way in the Last Frontier.

Staying Safe: Wildlife Encounters and Outdoor Precautions

Alaska's untamed wilderness presents unique challenges and opportunities for outdoor enthusiasts. By being prepared and following essential safety guidelines, you can minimize risks and ensure a safe and enjoyable experience.

Here's a comprehensive look at bear safety and additional tips for outdoor activities:

Bear Safety: Coexisting with Alaska's Wildlife

Understanding Bear Behavior:
Alaska is home to both brown bears (grizzlies) and black bears. Familiarize yourself with their behavior, habits, and signs of activity, such as tracks, scat, and diggings. Bears are generally solitary creatures and prefer to avoid humans. However, they can be attracted to food, especially during certain seasons.

Proper Food Storage:
- **In developed campgrounds:** Store all food, toiletries, and scented items in bear-resistant containers or lockers provided by the campground.
- **In backcountry areas:** Use bear-resistant canisters or hang food bags at least 10 feet off the ground and 4 feet away from tree trunks.
- Never leave food or scented items unattended in your tent or vehicle.

Hiking Precautions:
- **Make noise:** Talk, sing, or clap your hands periodically to alert bears to your presence and avoid surprising them.

- **Travel in groups:** There's safety in numbers. Hiking with others reduces the risk of bear encounters.
- **Be aware of your surroundings:** Watch for signs of bear activity and avoid hiking at dawn or dusk, when bears are most active.
- **Carry bear spray**: Bear spray is an effective deterrent in case of a close encounter. Know how to use it properly and keep it readily accessible.

Bear Spray Usage:
- **If a bear approaches:** Stand your ground, speak calmly, and slowly back away if possible. If the bear continues to approach, use bear spray when it's within 30-60 feet.
- **Aim for the face:** Spray a short burst directly at the bear's face, focusing on the eyes and nose.
- **Be prepared to reapply:** If the bear continues to charge, be ready to spray again.

Additional Safety Tips for Outdoor Activities:
Hiking:
- **Plan your route:** Research trail conditions, difficulty levels, and estimated hiking times.

- **Check weather forecasts:** Be prepared for changing weather, especially in mountainous areas.
- **Let someone know your itinerary:** Inform a friend or family member of your planned route and expected return time.
- **Carry essentials:** Pack a map, compass, first-aid kit, extra food and water, and appropriate clothing for the conditions.
- **Stay on designated trails:** Avoid venturing off-trail to minimize the risk of getting lost or encountering hazards.

Kayaking and Canoeing:

- **Wear a life jacket:** Always wear a properly fitted life jacket, regardless of your swimming ability.
- **Paddle with a partner:** Never paddle alone. It's safer and more enjoyable to share the experience.
- **Check weather and tides:** Be aware of changing weather conditions and tidal currents, especially in open waters.
- **File a float plan:** Let someone know your itinerary and expected return time.
- **Dress for the water:** Wear a wetsuit or drysuit, even in summer, as water temperatures can be cold.

Driving in Remote Areas:

- **Ensure your vehicle is in good condition:** Check tires, brakes, and fluids before embarking on a long drive.
- **Carry a spare tire and emergency supplies:** Be prepared for flat tires, breakdowns, or unexpected delays.
- **Fuel up frequently:** Gas stations can be sparse in remote areas, so fill up whenever possible.
- **Drive cautiously:** Be aware of wildlife, changing weather, and road conditions.
- **Let someone know your route and estimated arrival time:** Inform a friend or family member of your travel plans.

General Safety Tips:

- **Be prepared for changing weather:** Alaska's weather can be unpredictable, so pack layers and be ready for rain, snow, or sunshine.
- **Protect yourself from the sun:** Wear sunscreen, sunglasses, and a hat, even on cloudy days.
- **Stay hydrated:** Drink plenty of water, especially during outdoor activities.
- **Be aware of your surroundings:** Pay attention to your surroundings and be mindful of potential hazards, such as cliffs, fast-moving water, and wildlife.
- **Respect the environment**: Stay on designated trails, avoid disturbing wildlife, and leave no trace.

By following these safety guidelines and being prepared for the challenges of Alaska's wilderness, you can enjoy a safe and rewarding adventure in the Last Frontier. Remember, safety is paramount, and a little preparation goes a long way in ensuring a memorable and enjoyable experience.

Money Matters: Budgeting and Tipping

Alaska, with its remote location and vast wilderness, can be a more expensive destination than some. However, with careful planning and smart budgeting, you can create an unforgettable trip without breaking the bank. Here's a breakdown of typical costs and tips for saving money:

Transportation:

- **Airfare:** Airfare can vary greatly depending on your origin, travel dates, and airline. Expect to pay anywhere from $500 to $1500+ for a round-trip ticket during peak season.

- **Cruises:** Cruise prices vary based on the cruise line, itinerary, cabin type, and length of the trip. Budget for $1000-$5000+ per person for a 7-day Inside Passage cruise.
- **Rental Car:** Daily car rental rates range from $50 to $150+, depending on the vehicle type and season. Factor in additional costs for gas, which can be higher in remote areas.
- **Alaska Railroad:** Train fares vary depending on the route and class of service. Expect to pay $100-$300+ for a one-way ticket between major cities.
- **Ferries:** Ferry fares depend on the route and vessel type. Budget for $50-$200+ per person for a one-way trip.

Accommodation:
- **Camping:** The most budget-friendly option, with campground fees ranging from $10 to $30 per night.
- **Hostels:** Dormitory beds typically cost $25-$40 per night, while private rooms can range from $60-$100+.
- **Hotels and Motels**: Expect to pay $100-$250+ per night for a standard room in a hotel or motel, with prices higher in popular tourist areas.
- **Lodges and Resorts:** Lodges and resorts offer a more luxurious experience, with prices ranging from $200 to $500+ per night, depending on the location and amenities.

Activities:
- **National Park** Entrance Fees: Most national parks charge entrance fees, typically around $15-$30 per vehicle or $10-$15 per person. Consider purchasing an annual pass if you plan to visit multiple parks.
- **Guided Tours and Excursions:** Prices vary depending on the activity and duration. Budget for $50-$200+ per person for popular tours like whale watching, glacier trekking, or flightseeing.
- **Wildlife Viewing:** Some wildlife viewing opportunities are free, such as spotting animals along roadsides or in national parks. Guided tours can range from $50-$200+ per person.
- **Outdoor Activities:** Many outdoor activities, like hiking, kayaking, and fishing, can be enjoyed for free or with minimal gear rental costs.

Dining:
- **Restaurants:** Expect to pay $15-$30+ per person for a meal at a casual restaurant, with prices higher in fine dining establishments.
- **Grocery Stores:** Save money by stocking up on groceries and preparing your own meals, especially if you're staying in accommodations with kitchen facilities.
- **Food Trucks and Street Vendors:** Find affordable and delicious local eats from food trucks and street vendors, especially in larger cities.

Tipping:
- **Restaurants:** Tipping 15-20% is customary for good service.
- **Tour Guides and Drivers:** Tip $5-$10 per person for a half-day tour or $10-$20 for a full-day tour.
- **Bellhops and Housekeeping Staff:** Tip $1-$2 per bag for bellhops and $2-$5 per day for housekeeping staff.

Currency Exchange and Credit Cards:
- **Currency:** The US dollar is the official currency in Alaska.
- **Credit Cards:** Credit cards are widely accepted in most establishments, including hotels, restaurants, and tour operators.
- **ATMs:** ATMs are readily available in towns and cities throughout Alaska.
- **Cash:** It's advisable to carry some cash, especially for smaller businesses, remote areas, and tipping.

Budgeting Tips:
- **Travel during shoulder seasons:** May and September offer lower prices and fewer crowds than peak summer months.
- **Consider camping or staying in hostels:** These options provide significant savings on accommodation costs.
- **Cook your own meals:** Utilize kitchen facilities in your accommodation or pack picnic lunches for day trips.
- **Take advantage of free activities:** Hiking, wildlife viewing in national parks, and exploring local communities are all enjoyable and budget-friendly options.

- **Purchase an annual park pass**: If you plan to visit multiple national parks, an annual pass can save you money on entrance fees.
- **Research discounts and deals:** Look for discounts for seniors, students, military personnel, or AAA members.

By planning carefully, utilizing these budgeting tips, and prioritizing your must-do experiences, you can create an unforgettable Alaskan adventure that fits your budget and leaves you with cherished memories.

Communication and Connectivity: Staying in Touch

While Alaska's vast wilderness offers unparalleled beauty and tranquility, it also presents unique challenges when it comes to staying connected. Cell phone coverage and internet access can be limited or non-existent in remote areas, making communication and staying informed crucial aspects of trip planning. Here's what you need to know:

Challenges of Staying Connected:
- **Limited Cell Phone Coverage:** While major cities and towns generally have reliable cell phone coverage, venturing into national parks, remote areas, or smaller communities can result in spotty or no service.

- **Sparse Wi-Fi Availability:** Public Wi-Fi is not as widespread as in urban areas. Some hotels, cafes, and visitor centers may offer Wi-Fi, but it's not guaranteed in remote locations.
- **Satellite Dependence:** In extremely remote areas, communication relies on satellite phones or specialized communication devices, which can be expensive and require specific knowledge for operation.

Tips for Finding Wi-Fi:
- **Public Libraries:** Many public libraries offer free Wi-Fi access, making them a great option for checking emails or browsing the internet.
- **Visitor Centers:** National park visitor centers and some private lodges may offer Wi-Fi, though bandwidth may be limited during peak season.
- **Cafes and Restaurants:** Some cafes and restaurants offer Wi-Fi for customers, particularly in larger towns and cities.
- **Consider a Portable Wi-Fi Hotspot:** If you need reliable internet access on the go, a portable Wi-Fi hotspot can be a worthwhile investment.

Using Cell Phones:
- **Check Coverage Maps:** Before your trip, consult coverage maps from your cell phone provider to understand potential service limitations in the areas you'll be visiting.

- **Consider a Local SIM Card:** If you'll be spending extended time in Alaska, purchasing a local SIM card with a prepaid plan might be a cost-effective option for calling and texting.
- **Download Offline Maps and Information:** Save important maps, directions, and travel information on your phone before heading to areas with limited connectivity.
- **Use Wi-Fi Calling:** If your phone and carrier support it, enable Wi-Fi calling to make and receive calls using available Wi-Fi networks.

Communicating in Emergencies:
- **Satellite Phones:** For venturing into extremely remote areas without cell phone coverage, consider renting or purchasing a satellite phone for emergency communication.
- **Personal Locator Beacons (PLBs):** These devices can send an SOS signal with your location to search and rescue teams in case of an emergency.
- **Inform Others of Your Itinerary**: Always let someone know your planned route, expected return time, and any changes to your itinerary.
- **Be Prepared:** Pack essential safety gear, such as a first-aid kit, extra food and water, and a map and compass, especially when venturing into remote areas.

Remember:
- **Embrace the Disconnect:** While staying connected is important for safety and convenience, also embrace the opportunity to disconnect and fully immerse yourself in Alaska's natural beauty.
- **Plan Ahead:** Research communication options in the areas you'll be visiting and pack accordingly.
- **Prioritize Safety**: Always prioritize safety when exploring Alaska's wilderness. Be prepared for limited connectivity and carry essential communication tools for emergencies.

By understanding the challenges of staying connected in remote areas and following these tips, you can navigate Alaska's vast landscapes with confidence and ensure a safe and enjoyable adventure.

Respecting Local Culture and Environment: Responsible Travel

Alaska's pristine wilderness and rich cultural heritage are treasures to be cherished and protected. As a visitor, embracing responsible travel practices and minimizing your impact on the environment and local communities is essential.

Environmental Stewardship:
- **Leave No Trace**: Pack out everything you pack in, including food scraps, trash, and even biodegradable items like apple cores and banana peels. These can attract wildlife and disrupt the natural ecosystem.
- **Stay on Designated Trails:** Avoid trampling vegetation and disturbing fragile habitats by sticking to established trails.
- **Minimize Campfire Impact**: Use existing fire rings or camp stoves whenever possible. If building a fire, keep it small and contained, and ensure it's fully extinguished before leaving.
- **Respect Wildlife and Their Habitats:** Observe wildlife from a safe distance and never approach or feed them. Avoid disturbing nesting areas or den sites.
- **Conserve Water:** Use water sparingly, especially in remote areas where resources may be limited.

Cultural Sensitivity:
- **Learn about Alaska Native Cultures:** Take time to understand the diverse cultures and traditions of Alaska's indigenous peoples. Visit cultural centers, attend events, and engage in respectful dialogue with local residents.

- **Ask Permission Before Photographing:** Always ask permission before taking photos of people, especially Alaska Natives. Respect their privacy and cultural sensitivities.
- **Support Local Businesses:** Purchase authentic arts and crafts directly from Alaska Native artisans, and choose locally-owned businesses and tour operators whenever possible.
- **Be Mindful of Traditional Practices:** Some areas may have restrictions on certain activities, such as fishing or harvesting plants. Respect these customs and traditions.
- **Embrace the Alaskan Spirit:** Be open-minded, curious, and respectful of the local way of life. Embrace the slower pace, the connection to nature, and the unique cultural experiences that Alaska offers.

Supporting Sustainable Tourism:

- **Choose Eco-Friendly Tour Operators:** Seek out tour operators committed to sustainable practices, such as minimizing environmental impact, supporting local communities, and educating visitors about responsible travel.
- **Minimize Carbon Footprint:** Consider carbon offset programs or choose transportation options with lower emissions, such as trains or ferries.
- **Reduce Waste:** Bring a reusable water bottle, coffee mug, and shopping bag to minimize single-use plastics.
- **Support Conservation Efforts:** Donate to organizations working to protect Alaska's wildlife and natural resources.
- **Leave Positive Reviews:** Share your positive experiences with eco-friendly businesses and tour operators to encourage others to support sustainable tourism.

Remember:

Alaska's wilderness and cultures are fragile and precious. Your choices as a traveler can make a difference in preserving them for future generations. By practicing responsible travel, you not only protect Alaska's natural and cultural treasures but also enhance your own experience. Leave Alaska better than you found it, and encourage others to do the same.

CHAPTER 6

Itineraries for Every Interest

One size doesn't fit all when it comes to Alaska trips. Whether you're a hiker, a foodie, or just want to relax and take in the views, we've got you covered.

The Classic Alaska Itinerary: Hitting the Highlights

This 7-day itinerary showcases Alaska's most iconic destinations and experiences, offering a perfect blend of natural wonders, wildlife encounters, and cultural immersion.

Day 1: Anchorage Arrival
Arrive in Anchorage, Alaska's largest city, and settle into your accommodations. Take a stroll along the Tony Knowles Coastal Trail for stunning views of Cook Inlet and the Chugach Mountains. Visit the Anchorage Museum to learn about Alaska's art, history, and natural wonders.

Day 2: Anchorage to Seward and Kenai Fjords National Park

Embark on a scenic drive along the Seward Highway, marveling at glaciers, mountains, and waterfalls. Arrive in Seward, a charming coastal town nestled on Resurrection Bay. Take a boat tour in Kenai Fjords National Park, witnessing tidewater glaciers, abundant marine life, and breathtaking scenery.

Day 3: Seward to Denali National Park

Enjoy a leisurely morning in Seward, perhaps visiting the Alaska SeaLife Center or hiking to Exit Glacier. Board the Alaska Railroad for a scenic train journey to Denali National Park. Settle into your accommodations near the park entrance and prepare for wildlife adventures.

Day 4: Denali National Park Exploration

Embark on a narrated bus tour deep into Denali National Park, keeping your eyes peeled for bears, moose, caribou, and wolves. Hike a scenic trail like the Savage River Loop or the Horseshoe Lake Trail for stunning views and a chance to experience the park's wilderness firsthand.

Day 5: Denali to Fairbanks

Take a morning bus tour or hike in Denali before departing for Fairbanks. Board the Alaska Railroad for another scenic train journey, this time through the heart of Alaska's Interior. Arrive in Fairbanks, the "Golden Heart City," and check into your accommodations.

Day 6: Fairbanks and Surroundings

Visit the University of Alaska Museum of the North to learn about Alaska's natural and cultural history. Explore Pioneer Park, a living history museum showcasing the gold rush era. If time permits, take a scenic drive to Chena Hot Springs Resort for a relaxing soak in natural hot springs.

Day 7: Fairbanks to Glacier Bay National Park (Optional)

For an extended adventure, take a scenic flightseeing tour to Glacier Bay National Park, witnessing tidewater glaciers, breathtaking fjords, and abundant marine life from the air. If flightseeing isn't possible, enjoy a final day exploring Fairbanks or the surrounding areas.

Day 8: Departure

Depart from Fairbanks International Airport or connect to your onward destination, carrying with you cherished memories of your classic Alaskan adventure. This itinerary offers a taste of Alaska's most iconic destinations and experiences. Remember, you can customize this plan to fit your interests and time constraints. Add extra days for in-depth exploration, choose alternative activities, or simply relax and soak in the natural beauty of the Last Frontier.

No matter how you tailor your trip, this classic Alaska itinerary promises an unforgettable journey through a land of breathtaking scenery, abundant wildlife, and rich cultural heritage.

Calling all intrepid adventurers! This 7-day itinerary is designed for those seeking an immersive experience in Alaska's remote and untamed wilderness. Prepare to embark on a journey of discovery, where backpacking, kayaking, and stays in secluded lodges reveal the raw beauty and untamed spirit of the Last Frontier.

Day 1: Anchorage to Wrangell-St. Elias National Park

Arrive in Anchorage and pick up your rental car or arrange transportation to McCarthy, the gateway to Wrangell-St. Elias National Park. The drive to McCarthy is a scenic adventure in itself, winding through breathtaking landscapes and offering glimpses of wildlife. Settle into your accommodations in McCarthy or nearby Kennecott, a historic mining town turned ghost town.

Day 2-3: Backpacking in Wrangell-St. Elias

Embark on a multi-day backpacking trip into the heart of Wrangell-St. Elias, the largest national park in the United States.

Choose from a variety of trails, ranging from moderate to challenging, and experience the solitude and grandeur of this vast wilderness. Hike amidst towering mountains, glaciers, and pristine valleys, encountering wildlife and immersing yourself in the untouched beauty of the park.

Day 4: McCarthy to Valdez
Return to McCarthy and drive or take a shuttle to Chitina, where you'll catch a scenic flight to Valdez, nestled on the shores of Prince William Sound. Settle into your accommodations in Valdez and enjoy the town's picturesque harbor and surrounding mountains.

Day 5-6: Kayaking in Prince William Sound
Embark on a multi-day kayaking expedition in Prince William Sound, paddling through calm waters amidst towering glaciers, forested islands, and abundant marine life. Camp on secluded beaches, witness the power of calving glaciers, and encounter whales, sea otters, and seals in their natural habitat. Experienced guides will lead you through this pristine wilderness, ensuring a safe and unforgettable adventure.

Day 7: Valdez Departure

Enjoy a final morning in Valdez, perhaps taking a hike or exploring the town's shops and restaurants. Depart from Valdez via a scenic flight or continue your Alaskan journey by road or ferry.

Additional Tips for Wilderness Explorers:

- **Be prepared for challenging conditions:** Weather in Alaska can change rapidly, and remote areas can be unpredictable. Pack appropriate gear, including rain gear, warm layers, and sturdy footwear.
- **Leave no trace:** Practice Leave No Trace principles to minimize your impact on the environment. Pack out all trash and avoid disturbing wildlife or their habitats.
- **Be bear aware:** Take precautions to avoid bear encounters, including storing food properly and making noise while hiking.
- **Travel with experienced guides:** For backpacking and kayaking trips in remote areas, consider hiring experienced guides who can provide valuable knowledge, safety instruction, and logistical support.
- **Embrace the unexpected:** Be flexible and adaptable, as weather conditions or unforeseen circumstances may require changes to your itinerary.

This Wilderness Explorer Itinerary offers a glimpse into Alaska's most remote and awe-inspiring landscapes. By venturing off the beaten path and embracing the challenges and rewards of wilderness travel, you'll create an unforgettable adventure that will stay with you long after you leave the Last Frontier.

The Cultural Immersion Itinerary: Experiencing Local Life

This immersive 7-day journey invites you to connect with the heart and soul of Alaska, delving into the rich tapestry of Alaska Native cultures and traditions.

Through museum visits, cultural events, and interactions with local communities, you'll gain a deeper appreciation for the enduring spirit and artistic expressions of Alaska's indigenous peoples.

Day 1: Anchorage Arrival and Cultural Exploration

Arrive in Anchorage and settle into your accommodations. Visit the Alaska Native Heritage Center, a living museum showcasing the traditions and contemporary arts of Alaska's 11 major cultural groups. Explore traditional dwellings, witness captivating dance performances, and interact with knowledgeable cultural interpreters. Enjoy a traditional Alaskan dinner at a local restaurant, savoring the flavors of indigenous cuisine.

Day 2: Anchorage to Kenai Peninsula and the Alutiiq Museum

Embark on a scenic drive south along the Seward Highway to the Kenai Peninsula. Visit the Alutiiq Museum in Kodiak, dedicated to preserving and sharing the history and culture of the Alutiiq people. Explore exhibits showcasing traditional artifacts, archaeological finds, and contemporary artwork. Engage in a cultural workshop, such as basket weaving or drum making, led by local artisans.

Day 3: Kenai Peninsula to Homer and the Pratt Museum

Continue your journey along the Kenai Peninsula to the picturesque town of Homer, known for its stunning views of Kachemak Bay and vibrant arts community.

Visit the Pratt Museum, which highlights the natural and cultural history of the Kenai Peninsula. Explore exhibits on local wildlife, geology, and the traditions of the Dena'ina people. Attend a cultural performance or storytelling event at the Bunnell Street Arts Center.

Day 4: Homer to Juneau and the Sealaska Heritage Institute
Fly from Homer to Juneau, the capital city of Alaska. Immerse yourself in the rich heritage of Southeast Alaska's Tlingit, Haida, and Tsimshian cultures at the Sealaska Heritage Institute. Admire traditional regalia, learn about clan histories, and witness the artistry of contemporary Native artists. Take a guided tour of Juneau's historic downtown, exploring landmarks like St. Nicholas Russian Orthodox Church and the Alaska State Capitol.

Day 5: Juneau and Tlingit Culture
Visit the Tlingit Clan House, a traditional gathering place where you can learn about clan structures, social customs, and the importance of oral history. Take a walk through the Juneau-Douglas City Museum, showcasing the history of the region from the Tlingit era to the present day. Attend a traditional dance performance or storytelling session at the Walter Soboleff Building.

Day 6: Juneau to Ketchikan and Totem Poles
Take a scenic ferry ride or flight from Juneau to Ketchikan, known for its vibrant Tlingit culture and abundance of totem poles. Explore the Totem Heritage Center, home to a collection of restored totem poles and a carving shed where you can witness artists at work. Wander through Saxman Native Village, admiring the impressive collection of totem poles and learning about Tlingit traditions.

Day 7: Ketchikan and Departure
Enjoy a final morning in Ketchikan, perhaps taking a guided tour of the Tongass National Forest or visiting the Southeast Alaska Discovery Center. Depart from Ketchikan International Airport, carrying with you a deeper understanding and appreciation for Alaska's rich indigenous cultures.

The Family-Friendly Itinerary: Keeping Everyone Happy

Embark on an unforgettable journey through Alaska with this family-friendly itinerary, carefully curated to balance fun, adventure, and educational experiences that will captivate both young and old. From thrilling wildlife encounters to scenic train rides and interactive museums, this 7-day journey promises to create lasting memories for the whole family.

Day 1: Anchorage Arrival and Wildlife Wonders
Arrive in Anchorage, Alaska's largest city, and settle into your family-friendly accommodations. Head to the Alaska Wildlife Conservation Center, where you can witness rescued and rehabilitated Alaskan animals in spacious natural habitats. Take a scenic drive or guided tour through the center, spotting bears, moose, wolves, and more.

Day 2: Anchorage to Seward and Kenai Fjords National Park
Embark on a scenic drive along the Seward Highway, marveling at the stunning views of Turnagain Arm, glaciers, and mountains.

Arrive in Seward, a charming coastal town nestled on Resurrection Bay. Take a family-friendly boat tour in Kenai Fjords National Park, where you can witness tidewater glaciers, playful sea otters, and perhaps even breaching whales.

Day 3: Seward to Denali National Park
Enjoy a leisurely morning in Seward, perhaps visiting the Alaska SeaLife Center to learn about marine life and witness rescued animals. Board the Alaska Railroad for a scenic train journey to Denali National Park, offering breathtaking views of the Alaskan wilderness. Arrive in Denali and check into your accommodations near the park entrance.

Day 4: Denali National Park Exploration
Embark on a narrated bus tour deep into Denali National Park, keeping an eye out for bears, moose, caribou, and other iconic wildlife. Choose a shorter tour option, like the Tundra Wilderness Tour, to keep younger children engaged. Hike a family-friendly trail, such as the Horseshoe Lake Trail or the Savage River Loop, for stunning views and a chance to connect with nature.

Day 5: Denali to Fairbanks
Take a morning bus tour or hike in Denali before departing for Fairbanks. Board the Alaska Railroad for another scenic train journey, this time through the heart of Alaska's Interior. Arrive in Fairbanks, the "Golden Heart City," and check into your accommodations.

Day 6: Fairbanks Fun and Discovery
Visit the University of Alaska Museum of the North, where interactive exhibits and captivating displays bring Alaska's natural and cultural history to life. Explore Pioneer Park, a living history museum showcasing the gold rush era. Pan for gold, ride the carousel, and learn about Alaska's pioneering spirit. In the evening, head to Creamer's Field Migratory Waterfowl Refuge for a chance to see Sandhill Cranes and other birds in their natural habitat.

Day 7: Fairbanks Departure or Extended Adventure

If time allows, consider extending your trip with a visit to Chena Hot Springs Resort, where you can soak in natural hot springs, visit an ice museum, and even try your hand at dog sledding or snowmobiling (depending on the season). Otherwise, depart from Fairbanks International Airport, carrying with you cherished memories of your Alaskan family adventure.

Remember:

Pack plenty of snacks and activities for long drives and train rides. Choose accommodations with family-friendly amenities like pools, playgrounds, or game rooms. Be flexible and adjust your itinerary based on your children's energy levels and interests. Embrace the spontaneity of travel and allow for unexpected detours and discoveries. Most importantly, have fun and create lasting memories with your loved ones in the breathtaking wilderness of Alaska!

The Budget Traveler's Itinerary: Making the Most of Your Money

Alaska's majestic beauty doesn't have to come with a hefty price tag. With a little planning and resourcefulness, you can experience the wonders of the Last Frontier without breaking the bank.

This 7-day budget-friendly itinerary focuses on affordable accommodations, transportation options, and free or low-cost activities, ensuring you get the most out of your Alaskan adventure.

Day 1: Anchorage Arrival and Exploring on Foot

Arrive in Anchorage and opt for budget-friendly accommodations like a hostel or a campground. Explore the city on foot, taking advantage of free attractions like the Tony Knowles Coastal Trail, Earthquake Park, and the Anchorage Market.

Day 2: Chugach State Park and Potter Marsh

Rent a bike or utilize public transportation to access Chugach State Park, a vast wilderness area with stunning hiking trails and scenic vistas. Hike the popular Flattop Mountain trail for panoramic views of Anchorage and the surrounding mountains. Visit Potter Marsh, a boardwalk trail through a scenic wetland teeming with birdlife.

Day 3: Seward Highway and Kenai Peninsula

Take a scenic bus tour or carpool along the Seward Highway, stopping at viewpoints and roadside attractions to enjoy the stunning scenery. Explore the Kenai Peninsula, home to charming towns, glaciers, and abundant wildlife. Consider camping or staying in a budget-friendly motel in Seward or Soldotna.

Day 4: Hiking and Wildlife Viewing in Kenai Fjords National Park

Hike the Exit Glacier Trail in Kenai Fjords National Park for stunning views of the glacier and its surrounding landscapes. Visit the Alaska SeaLife Center in Seward to learn about marine life and witness rescued animals. Consider purchasing a multi-day pass for discounted admission. Drive or take a bus to the Kenai National Wildlife Refuge for opportunities to spot moose, bears, and other wildlife.

Day 5: Scenic Drive to Talkeetna

Embark on a scenic drive to the charming town of Talkeetna, nestled at the base of Denali. Stay in a budget-friendly lodge or campground and enjoy the town's unique shops, art galleries, and restaurants. Hike the trails around Talkeetna for stunning views of Denali and the surrounding mountains.

Day 6: Denali National Park on a Budget

Take a shuttle bus into Denali National Park, opting for a shorter, more affordable tour like the Tundra Wilderness Tour. Pack a picnic lunch and snacks to save on dining costs within the park. Hike the trails near the park entrance, such as the Savage River Loop or the Horseshoe Lake Trail, for scenic views and potential wildlife encounters.

Day 7: Fairbanks and the Aurora Borealis

Take a scenic train ride or bus from Denali to Fairbanks, the "Golden Heart City." Stay in a hostel or budget hotel in Fairbanks and explore its attractions, such as Pioneer Park and the University of Alaska Museum of the North. If visiting during the Aurora season (September-April), venture outside the city for optimal Northern Lights viewing opportunities. Consider joining a budget-friendly aurora viewing tour or finding a secluded spot away from city lights.

Remember:

Embrace the outdoors: Alaska's natural beauty is its greatest asset, and many of its most rewarding experiences are free. Hiking, camping, wildlife viewing, and exploring local communities are all fantastic ways to experience the state without spending a fortune.

- **Cook your meals:** Take advantage of kitchen facilities in your accommodations or pack picnic lunches to save on dining costs.
- **Utilize public transportation:** Consider taking buses or shuttles instead of renting a car, especially if you're traveling solo or in a small group.
- **Look for discounts and deals**: Many attractions, tours, and businesses offer discounts for seniors, students, military personnel, or AAA members. Research these options in advance to save money.
- **Pack smart:** Bring essential gear like rain gear, hiking boots, and a reusable water bottle to avoid unnecessary expenses.

By planning carefully, utilizing these budget-friendly tips, and embracing the spirit of adventure, you can experience the wonders of Alaska without exceeding your financial limits.Remember, the most valuable souvenirs are the memories you create and the experiences you share.

APPENDIX

Essential Alaskan Phrases

While English is widely spoken in Alaska, learning a few phrases in the local indigenous languages demonstrates respect for the rich cultural heritage and can enhance your interactions with local communities. Here's a brief guide to essential phrases in some of the major Alaska Native languages:

Greetings:
General:
- Hello: "Xaat sitee" (Tlingit), "Háw'aa" (Haida), "Yá'át'ééh" (Navajo)
- Goodbye: "Gunalchéesh" (Tlingit), "Ła gúusdée" (Haida), "Hágoónee'" (Navajo)
- Thank you: "Gunalchéesh" (Tlingit), "Haw'aa" (Haida), "Ahéhee'" (Navajo)
- Please: "Please" is often understood in English or can be conveyed through gestures and tone.

Specific Greetings:
- Good morning: "Góod eiy sángaa" (Tlingit)
- Good afternoon: "Góod tl'a sángaa" (Tlingit)
- Good evening: "Góod dís sángaa" (Tlingit)

Basic Conversation Starters:
- How are you?: "Wáa sá iyatee?" (Tlingit), "Nang kingaan?" (Haida)
- My name is...: "Ax ___ wé du." (Tlingit), "Laa ___ xaaygang." (Haida)
- What is your name?: "Wáa hín du?" (Tlingit), "Nang kingaan?" (Haida)

- I am from...: "___ yáa ḵaa yáx̱." (Tlingit), "___ dít aa ḵáagang." (Haida)
- I don't understand: "Tlein ḵáa yax̱tutéeni." (Tlingit), "Gam hl dahgan." (Haida)
- Do you speak English?: "Wooshkee yanei English?" (Tlingit) "Łingalahaan sdang English?" (Haida)

Emergency Terms:
- Help!: "Yatee!" (Tlingit), "X̱áagu!" (Haida)
- I am lost: "X̱aakw sdéin." (Tlingit), "Tláa ḵáagang." (Haida)
- I am injured: "S'igeiyí ḵáa yei ḵaagú." (Tlingit), "X̱áagang gu ḵíinaagang." (Haida)
- Call the police: "Dooxóos s'eitikee." (Tlingit), "Kíl yahdaasgee." (Haida)
- Call an ambulance: "Aankháawu s'eitikee." (Tlingit), "Aankháawu yahdaasgee." (Haida)
- Note: These are just a few basic phrases. Many Alaska Native languages are endangered, so it's important to be patient and understanding when communicating with locals. Even attempting a few words shows respect and a willingness to learn about their culture.

Additional Tips:
- **Learn Pronunciation:** Alaska Native languages have unique sounds and pronunciations. Practice with online resources or language apps to ensure accurate communication.
- **Use Gestures and Body Language**: Non-verbal cues can often bridge language barriers. Smile, make eye contact, and use gestures to aid understanding.
- **Be Respectful:** Approach language learning with humility and respect. Avoid making assumptions or stereotypes about Alaska Native cultures.

By learning a few essential phrases and engaging in respectful dialogue, you'll deepen your connection with Alaska's indigenous communities and enrich your travel experience. Remember, even a small effort to communicate in the local language can go a long way in building bridges and fostering understanding.

Anchorage

SCAN THE QR CODE

- Open your device's camera app
- Point the camera at the QR code
- Ensure the QR code is within the frame and well-lit
- Wait for your device to recognize the QR code
- Once recognized, tap on the map and input for current location for direction and distance to the destination

Fairbanks

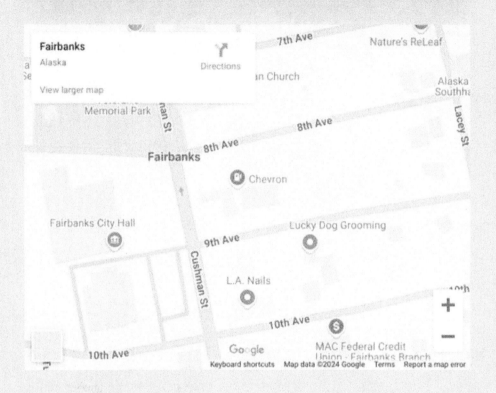

SCAN THE QR CODE

- Open your device's camera app
- Point the camera at the QR code
- Ensure the QR code is within the frame and well-lit
- Wait for your device to recognize the QR code
- Once recognized, tap on the map and input for current location for direction and distance to the destination

Juneau

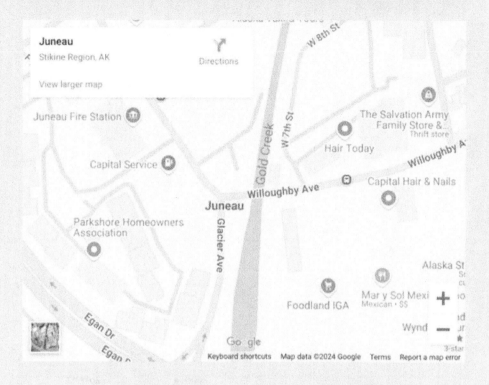

SCAN THE QR CODE

- Open your device's camera app
- Point the camera at the QR code
- Ensure the QR code is within the frame and well-lit
- Wait for your device to recognize the QR code
- Once recognized, tap on the map and input for current location for direction and distance to the destination

Seward

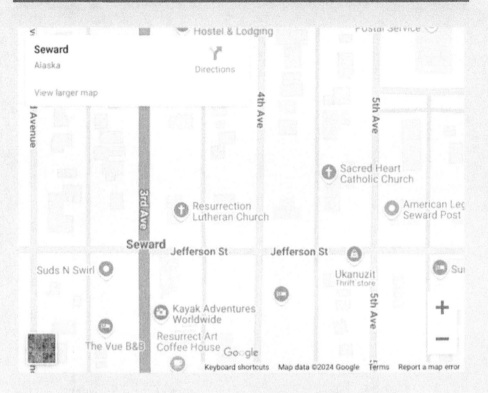

SCAN THE QR CODE

- Open your device's camera app
- Point the camera at the QR code
- Ensure the QR code is within the frame and well-lit
- Wait for your device to recognize the QR code
- Once recognized, tap on the map and input for current location for direction and distance to the destination

Homer

SCAN THE QR CODE

- Open your device's camera app
- Point the camera at the QR code
- Ensure the QR code is within the frame and well-lit
- Wait for your device to recognize the QR code
- Once recognized, tap on the map and input for current location for direction and distance to the destination

Denali National Park

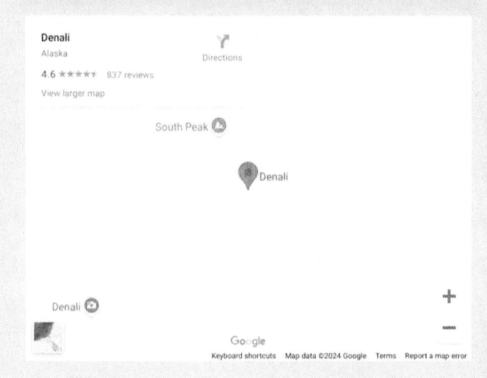

Denali
Alaska

4.6 ★★★★★ 837 reviews

View larger map

Directions

South Peak

Denali

Denali

Google

Keyboard shortcuts   Map data ©2024 Google   Terms   Report a map error

SCAN THE QR CODE

- Open your device's camera app
- Point the camera at the QR code
- Ensure the QR code is within the frame and well-lit
- Wait for your device to recognize the QR code
- Once recognized, tap on the map and input for current location for direction and distance to the destination

Kenai Fjords National Park

Kenai Fjords National Park

Seward, AK 99664

4.9 ★★★★★ 1,649 reviews

View larger map

Directions

Kenai Fjords
National Park

Google

Keyboard shortcuts   Map data ©2024 Google   Terms   Report a map error

SCAN THE QR CODE

- Open your device's camera app
- Point the camera at the QR code
- Ensure the QR code is within the frame and well-lit
- Wait for your device to recognize the QR code
- Once recognized, tap on the map and input for current location for direction and distance to the destination

Ketchikan

SCAN THE QR CODE

- Open your device's camera app
- Point the camera at the QR code
- Ensure the QR code is within the frame and well-lit
- Wait for your device to recognize the QR code
- Once recognized, tap on the map and input for current location for direction and distance to the destination

Sitka

SCAN THE QR CODE

- Open your device's camera app
- Point the camera at the QR code
- Ensure the QR code is within the frame and well-lit
- Wait for your device to recognize the QR code
- Once recognized, tap on the map and input for current location for direction and distance to the destination

Soldotna

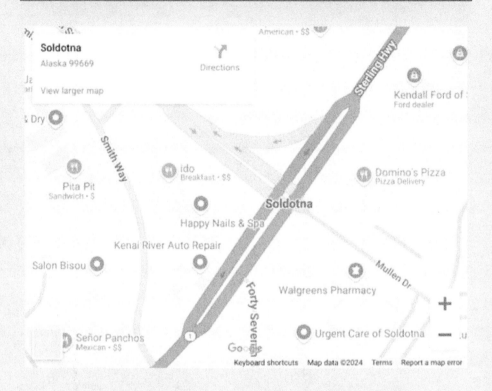

Soldotna
Alaska 99669

Directions

View larger map

Kendall Ford of :
Ford dealer

Domino's Pizza
Pizza Delivery

Pita Pit
Sandwich · $

ido
Breakfast · $$

Soldotna

Happy Nails & Spa

Kenai River Auto Repair

Salon Bisou

Walgreens Pharmacy

Señor Panchos
Mexican · $$

Urgent Care of Soldotna

Keyboard shortcuts   Map data ©2024   Terms   Report a map error

SCAN THE QR CODE

- Open your device's camera app
- Point the camera at the QR code
- Ensure the QR code is within the frame and well-lit
- Wait for your device to recognize the QR code
- Once recognized, tap on the map and input for current location for direction and distance to the destination

Skagway

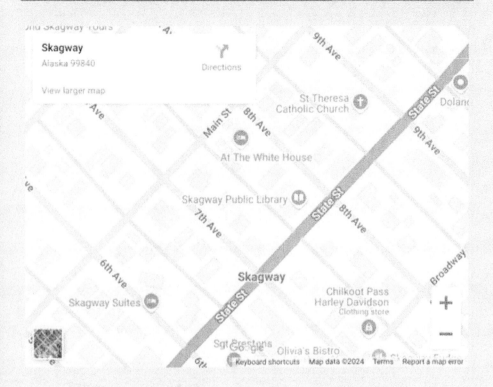

SCAN THE QR CODE

- Open your device's camera app
- Point the camera at the QR code
- Ensure the QR code is within the frame and well-lit
- Wait for your device to recognize the QR code
- Once recognized, tap on the map and input for current location for direction and distance to the destination

Valdez

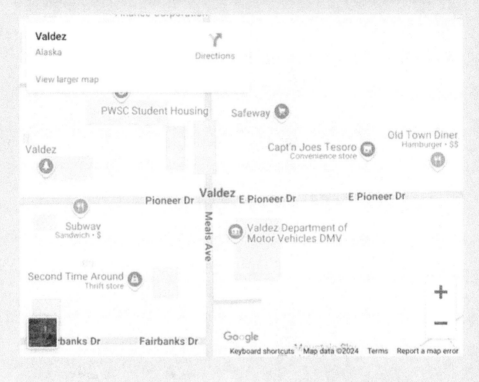

SCAN THE QR CODE

- Open your device's camera app
- Point the camera at the QR code
- Ensure the QR code is within the frame and well-lit
- Wait for your device to recognize the QR code
- Once recognized, tap on the map and input for current location for direction and distance to the destination

Talkeetna

Talkeetna
Alaska 99676

Directions

K2 Aviation

View larger map

Talkeetna

untaineering

S Terminal Ave

S Terminal Ave

Talkeetna Spur Rd

Google

Denali Fireside

Keyboard shortcuts   Map data ©2024 Google   Terms   Report a map error

SCAN THE QR CODE

- Open your device's camera app
- Point the camera at the QR code
- Ensure the QR code is within the frame and well-lit
- Wait for your device to recognize the QR code
- Once recognized, tap on the map and input for current location for direction and distance to the destination

ENHANCE YOUR JOURNEY WITH INTERACTIVE MAPS

Scan the QR codes on the maps throughout this guide to unlock a wealth of additional information, including:

- Interactive maps: Zoom in on specific regions and attractions for detailed navigation and exploration.
- Real-time updates: Get the latest information on weather conditions, road closures, and events happening near you.
- Exclusive content: Access bonus travel tips, insider recommendations, and hidden gems not found in the book.

To scan QR codes, simply download a free QR code reader app on your smartphone. We recommend using a reliable and user-friendly app such as:

- **QR CODE SCANNER & SCANNER APP** : AVAILABLE FOR BOTH IOS AND ANDROID DEVICES, THIS APP IS QUICK, EFFICIENT, AND OFFERS A SEAMLESS SCANNING EXPERIENCE.

By utilizing these interactive maps and QR codes, you can further personalize your Alaskan adventure and discover even more of what this beautiful city has to offer. Happy travels!

FROM THE AUTHOR

If this guide helped you uncover the hidden treasures of Alaska and create unforgettable memories, we'd love to hear about it! Your review on Amazon helps other adventurous travelers discover the magic of the beautiful city

Here's how to leave a review:
- Head to Amazon.com (or your local Amazon site).
- Search for the book by its title: "Alaska Travel Guide 2025: Essential tips for exploring the last frontier with ease"
- Once on the book's page, scroll down to the "Customer Reviews" section.
- Click on the button that says "Write a customer review".
- Give the book a star rating (hopefully 5!) and share your thoughts in the text box provided.
- Hit "Submit"!

It's that easy – and your feedback is invaluable to us!

MY TRAVEL PLAN

TRAVEL ITINERARY

Date: _____

S S M T W T F

Date:

Location:

Budget:

Trip To-do List

Daily Expenses

Daily Log

6 AM

7 AM

8 AM

9 AM

10 AM

11 AM

12 PM

1 PM

2 PM

3 PM

4 PM

5 PM

6 PM

7 PM

8 PM

NOTE:

Alaska Travel Guide

MY PACKING LIST

TRAVEL ITINERARY

Date: _____

S S M T W T F

THINGS TO PACK ⬤

- ◯
- ◯
- ◯
- ◯
- ◯
- ◯
- ◯
- ◯
- ◯
- ◯
- ◯
- ◯
- ◯
- ◯
- ◯
- ◯
- ◯
- ◯

ACCOMODATION

Name of Hotel

Location:

Check In Date:

Check Out Date:

Total Cost:

TRANSPORT

NOTES

PLACES TO VISIT

TRAVEL ITINERARY

Date: _____

S S M T W T F

Place	Visitor's Review
	☆☆☆☆☆☆☆☆☆☆
	☆☆☆☆☆☆☆☆☆☆
	☆☆☆☆☆☆☆☆☆☆
	☆☆☆☆☆☆☆☆☆☆
	☆☆☆☆☆☆☆☆☆☆
	☆☆☆☆☆☆☆☆☆☆
	☆☆☆☆☆☆☆☆☆☆
	☆☆☆☆☆☆☆☆☆☆
	☆☆☆☆☆☆☆☆☆☆
	☆☆☆☆☆☆☆☆☆☆
	☆☆☆☆☆☆☆☆☆☆
	☆☆☆☆☆☆☆☆☆☆
	☆☆☆☆☆☆☆☆☆☆
	☆☆☆☆☆☆☆☆☆☆

Notes

TRAVEL JOURNAL
TRAVEL REVIEW

Date: _____

S S M T W T F

Today's experience

THANK YOU

FOR
VISITING
ALASKA

ENJOY!